JAPAN'S KUMANO KODO PILGRIMAGE

About the Author

Originally from Melbourne, after graduating from university Kat moved to Japan, where she was an adventure tour guide and spent her time seeking out the local hotspots, eating *mochi,* and hiking whenever possible. 'A wise man climbs Mt Fuji; a fool climbs it twice' is a popular Japanese saying – so Kat climbed it seven times. From Japan she moved to Canada and then London, where she is now based. She quit her office job in 2013 to walk the Camino de Santiago and has never looked back. She has since completed numerous Caminos and walked over 10,000km around the world, including the Pacific Crest Trail and the Shikoku 88 Temple Pilgrimage, and is a registered Dual Pilgrim.

Other Cicerone guides by the author
The Camino Portugués

JAPAN'S KUMANO KODO PILGRIMAGE

THE UNESCO WORLD HERITAGE TREK

by Kat Davis

JUNIPER HOUSE, MURLEY MOSS,
OXENHOLME ROAD, KENDAL, CUMBRIA LA9 7RL
www.cicerone.co.uk

Printed in China on behalf of Latitude Press Ltd
All photographs are by the author unless otherwise stated.
A catalogue record for this book is available from the British Library.

 Route mapping by Lovell Johns www.lovelljohns.com
Contains OpenStreetMap.org data © OpenStreetMap contributors, CC-BY-SA. NASA relief data courtesy of ESRI

Updates to this Guide

While every effort is made by our authors to ensure the accuracy of guidebooks as they go to print, changes can occur during the lifetime of an edition. Any updates that we know of for this guide will be on the Cicerone website (www.cicerone.co.uk/972/updates), so please check before planning your trip. We also advise that you check information about such things as transport, accommodation and shops locally. Even rights of way can be altered over time.

The route maps in this guide are derived from publicly available data, databases and crowd-sourced data. As such they have not been through the detailed checking procedures that would generally be applied to a published map from an official mapping agency, although naturally we have reviewed them closely in the light of local knowledge as part of the preparation of this guide.

We are always grateful for information about any discrepancies between a guidebook and the facts on the ground, sent by email to updates@cicerone.co.uk or by post to Cicerone, Juniper House, Murley Moss, Oxenholme Road, Kendal, LA9 7RL.

Register your book: To sign up to receive free updates, special offers and GPX files where available, register your book at www.cicerone.co.uk.

Front cover: Hatenashi settlement (Kohechi, Stage 4)

CONTENTS

Tall one-directional cedar trees at the entrance to Tsugizakura-oji (Nakahechi, Stage 1)

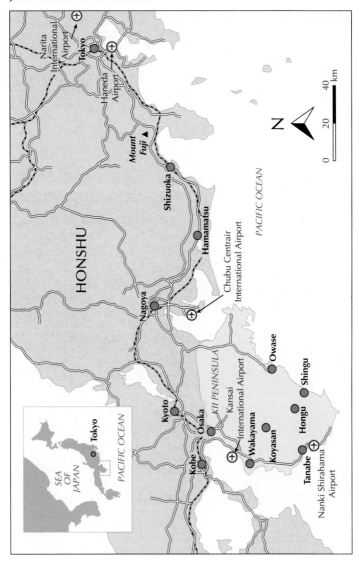

Symbols used on route maps

route
alternative route
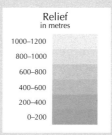

Relief
in metres

1000–1200
800–1000
600–800
400–600
200–400
0–200

(S) start point
(F) finish point
(SF) start/finish point
(S) alternative start point
(F) alternative finish point
woodland
station/railway

▲ peak
)(pass
≅ bridge
⊥ cemetery
☀ TV tower/antenna
• water feature
⌂ hotel/accommodation
campground
restaurant
café
toilets/WC
ATM
post office
supermarket/groceries
vending machine
bus station/bus stop
site/POI
viewpoint

⊛ police station
(H) hospital
⊕ medical (clinic)
⊕ pharmacy
❶ tourist information centre
☏ payphone
rest area/shelter
water supply
public baths

Waymarks

1 Hongu loop – Dainichi-goe waymarks
2 Hongu loop – Akagi-goe waymarks
9 Nakahechi waymarks
52 Nakahechi – Kogumotori-goe waymarks
26 Nakahechi – Ogumotori-goe waymarks
60 Koyasan – Choishi markers
1 Koyasan – Ri-ishi markers
20 Koyasan – Nyoninmichi waymarks
30 Kohechi – numbered Kannon statues
22 Iseji – Magose-toge waymarks
7 Iseji – Matsumoto-toge waymarks

SCALE: 1:50,000

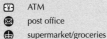
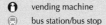

0 kilometres 0.5 1
0 miles 0.5

GPX files

GPX files for all routes can be downloaded for free at www.cicerone.co.uk/972/GPX.

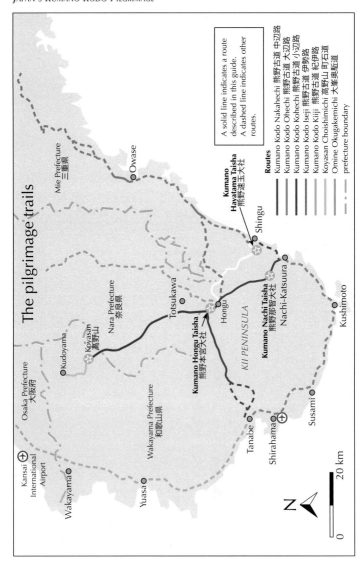

Springtime on the Kumano Kodo (Nakahechi, Stage 1)

x

Springtime on the Kumano Kodo (Nakahechi, Stage 1)

ROUTE SUMMARY TABLES

Hongu loop

Section	Start	Finish	Distance (km)	Ascent (m)	Descent (m)	Page
Dainichi-goe route	Kumano Hongu Taisha	Yunomine Onsen	2.8	240	185	98
Akagi-goe route	Yunomine Onsen	Funatama-jinja Shrine	5.7	415	275	102
Nakahechi route	Funatama-jinja Shrine	Kumano Hongu Taisha	8.2	220	415	103
Total	Kumano Hongu Taisha	Kumano Hongu Taisha	16.7	875	875	

Nakahechi

Stage	Start	Finish	Distance (km)	Ascent (m)	Descent (m)	Page
1	Takijiri-oji	Tsugizakura-oji, Nonaka	16.4	1205	765	113
2	Tsugizakura-oji, Nonaka	Kumano Hongu Taisha	20.6	820	1260	128
3 (Kogumotori-goe)	Ukegawa trailhead	Koguchi	12.6	665	650	137
4 (Ogumotori-goe)	Koguchi	Kumano Nachi Taisha	14.2	1180	895	145
Total	Takijiri-oji	Kumano Nachi Taisha	63.8	3870	3570	

Koyasan

Route	Start	Finish	Distance (km)	Ascent (m)	Descent (m)	Page
Choishimichi	Kudoyama station	Daimon gate, Koyasan	20.1	1145	395	152

Kohechi

Stage	Start	Finish	Distance (km)	Ascent (m)	Descent (m)	Page
1	Koyasan central tourist office	Omata bus stop	16.8	660	825	166
2	Omata bus stop	Miura-guchi bus stop	14	755	1020	173
3	Miura-guchi bus stop	Yanagimoto-bashi suspension bridge, Totsukawa Onsen	18.3	780	935	180
4	Yanagimoto-bashi suspension bridge	Kumano Hongu Taisha	14.3	1050	1100	190
Total	Koyasan central tourist office	Kumano Hongu Taisha	63.4	3245	3880	

Iseji highlights

Route	Start	Finish	Distance (km)	Ascent (m)	Descent (m)	Page
Magose-toge Pass	Aiga station	Owase station	6.7	325	335	200
Matsumoto-toge Pass	Odomari station	Arii station	4.9	125	130	209

13

Kumano Nachi Taisha

INTRODUCTION

Hatenashi settlement and a sea of mountains (Kohechi, Stage 4)

Imagine a journey in a remote, ancient and spiritual region of Japan. Hiking through an endless sea of mountains; tree-covered, with hidden valleys, waterfalls and traditional rural villages. After a day of invigorating walking, you've soaked in the steaming-hot *onsen*, dressed in a *yukata* and enjoyed a delicious meal of the freshest local produce in the company of strangers soon to be friends, before falling into a deep sleep on your futon.

The Kumano Kodo 熊野古道, literally 'old roads to Kumano' (also known as the Kumano Sankeimichi), is a network of pilgrimage trails that traverse the rugged mountains of the Kii Peninsula, due south of Kyoto,

to reach the three grand shrines of Kumano: Kumano Hongu Taisha, Kumano Hayatama Taisha and Kumano Nachi Taisha – known collectively as the Kumano Sanzan.

Koyasan 高野山, the high mountain basin where Kobo Daishi established his Shingon school of Esoteric Buddhism in AD816 and where he is said to be resting in eternal meditation, has been a major centre of pilgrimage for over 1200 years. This historic Buddhist complex is connected to the Kumano Sanzan via the Kumano Kodo Kohechi route.

In 2004, under the title 'Sacred Sites and Pilgrimage Routes in the Kii Mountain Range', Kumano Sanzan,

Koyasan and Yoshino & Omine and their associated pilgrimage trails were awarded UNESCO World Heritage Status. As such, the Kumano Kodo joined the Camino de Santiago as one of only two UNESCO-listed pilgrimages in the world, and hikers who complete both can register as 'Dual Pilgrims'. Whereas the Camino de Santiago is generally considered a long-distance route, the nature of the Kumano Kodo allows for pilgrimages of varying lengths, from single-day hikes to multi-week itineraries, depending on time and fitness.

HISTORY

Long known as a sacred site of nature worship and an 'abode of the gods', it was here in the ancient region of Kumano that the Hana-no-Iwaya boulder (see Iseji highlights – Matsumoto-toge Pass) was revered as the grave of Izanami-no-Mikoto, the goddess creator of Japan according to Japan's creation myth and the *Nihon Shoki* (*Chronicles of Japan*, AD720). Japan's oldest book, the *Kojiki* (*Record of Ancient Matters*, AD712), records that it was also here that the legendary Emperor Jimmu (around 660BC), a descendant of the sun goddess Amaterasu, landed in the south of the peninsula. He was guided over the mountains by the mythical Yatagarasu (three-legged crow) that was sent from heaven, and discovered Nachi Falls on his way to Yamato (modern-day Nara), where he established rule as the first emperor of Japan.

Buddhism was introduced to Japan in the sixth century and by the Heian period (794–1185) it had

Sacred Yatagarasu crow, Kumano Hongu Taisha

largely integrated with the indigenous Shinto religion, in what became known as *shinbutsu-shugo* (Shinto-Buddhist syncretism). The Shinto gods of Kumano came to be thought of as manifestations of Buddhist deities (Kumano Gongen). A complex, interwoven religious belief system emerged, combining Shintoism, Taoism (an ancient Chinese religion), Esoteric and Pure Land Buddhism (schools of Japanese Buddhism). Nature worship continued: Shugendo mountain ascetics (see glossary of religious terms below) saw the rugged terrain as the ideal site for their religious training in order to attain supernatural powers; Shingon esoteric priests saw the mountains as a place to attain enlightenment; and others considered the region the 'Buddhist pure land paradise on earth'.

It was 1100 years ago that pilgrimages to the Kumano Sanzan were popularised by imperial families and nobility. Starting with the former emperor Uda in 907, there were over 100 imperial pilgrimages, ending with the former emperor Kameyama in 1281. Large imperial processions set out from the ancient capital of Kyoto guided by *sendatsu* (Shugendo ascetics), stopping to rest and worship at the 99-*oji* (subsidiary shrines of the Kumano Sanzan). They continuously performed ritual purification rites intended to purify their sins, find salvation and be ritually reborn in the Buddhist pure land. The month-long return journeys were strenuous affairs

that were mostly undertaken on foot to accumulate religious merit. (No pain, no gain!) A number of diary accounts exist from these pilgrimages – notably the *Chuyuki* by Fujiwara Munetada, written in 1109, and the *Gokoki* by Fujiwara Teika, detailing former emperor Go-Toba's pilgrimage of 1201.

It was widely believed that with repeated pilgrimages and religious training, more merit could be accrued for the afterlife. Emperor Shirakawa (1053–1129) visited 12 times, Emperor Toba (1103–1156) 23 times, Emperor Go-Shirakawa (1127–1192) 33 times, Emperor Go-Toba (1180–1239) 29 times... (A stone memorial with the list of emperor and empress consort names and the number of pilgrimages each made can be seen in the grounds of Kumano Hayatama Taisha.)

The Kamakura period (1185–1333), named after the shogunate (military government) that was established in Kamakura and began seven centuries of military rule, marked the end of imperial pilgrimages and the beginning of pilgrimages by samurai warriors.

During the Muromachi period (1333–1573) the Kumano pilgrimage gained popularity with commoners, and the term '*ari no Kumano mode*' was coined, comparing the number of pilgrims to a 'procession of ants'. From the late 16th century the Kumano *bikuni* nuns and *hijiri* wandering priests were prolific, travelling around

Japan proselytising the Kumano faith using pilgrimage *mandalas* (iconography) as pictorial guides; these can be seen at the grand shrines. Pilgrimages to Ise-jingu Shrine and then onto the 33 Kannon (temple) pilgrimage of Western Japan (Saigoku Junrei) along the Kumano Kodo also gained momentum; Seiganto-ji Temple, next to Kumano Nachi Taisha, is the first of the 33 temples.

The Edo period (1603–1868) marked an era of stability throughout Japan and under the leadership of the Kishu Domain feudal lord, Tokugawa Yorinobu (1602–1671), the Kumano Kodo trails underwent an overhaul, with many of the flagstone paths and teahouse remains seen today dating from this time. While travel was generally restricted during this period, pilgrimages were an exception and continued to flourish.

Pilgrimages declined during the Meiji period (1868–1912), a turbulent time for religion in Japan: Shinto and Buddhism were separated by decree in 1868; Shugendo was banned as a superstitious religion (it's now allowed); Kumano Hongu Taisha's original shrine complex on a sandbank was destroyed in a devastating flood; and as a result of the Shrine Consolidation Policy (1906), many shrines were destroyed and their forests cut down. Thankfully, due to the foresight of Wakayama-born conservationist and botanist Minakata Kumagusu (1867–1941), a number of sites were saved, and after World War 2, in a bid to rebuild Japan, large areas were re-forested with cedar and cypress, shaping the mountains as we see them today.

Since the 2004 UNESCO World Heritage designation, the Kumano Kodo has once again witnessed a resurgence in the number of pilgrims. In 2015 the Kumano Kodo and Camino de Santiago were 'twinned', resulting in the 'Dual Pilgrim' programme.

JAPANESE SPIRITUALITY

'The way of the gods', **Shinto** 神道 is Japan's indigenous religion and worships *kami*. Shintoism has no founder or scriptures; it is a belief system that has been passed on through festivals, rituals and ceremonies and is thought to have been in existence since at least the Yayoi period (300BC–AD300). **Kami** 神 are gods or spirits, and there are so many that they're referred to as *yao-yorozu* (the eight million deities) and are believed to inhabit many things including rivers, rocks, trees, waterfalls, mountains, animals and people. **Torii** gates and the **shimenawa** rope are symbols of Shinto that denote the boundary between the sacred and secular worlds; the largest *torii* in Japan can be seen at Oyunohara (Hongu), and the *shimenawa* rope can, for example, be seen hung at the entrances to shrines, above Nachi Falls (Nachisan), around Gotobiki-iwa rock (Shingu) and draped across Hana-no-Iwaya boulder near Kumano City.

The three grand shrines of Kumano are examples of **Shinbutsu-shugo** 神仏習合 – Shinto/Buddhist syncretism. The **Kumano Gongen** 熊野権現 are the Kumano *kami* which are thought to be manifestations of Buddhist deities. There are 12 Kumano deities, although there are sometimes considered to be 13 with the inclusion of Kumano Nachi Taisha's Hiro Gongen. The **Kumano Sansho Gongen** 熊野三所権現 are the three main *kami* (and their Buddhist manifestations) who are enshrined at each of the grand shrines:

- Kumano Hongu Taisha – Ketsumiko-no-Okami (Amida Nyorai)
- Kumano Hayatama Taisha – Hayatama-no-Okami (Yakushi Nyorai)
- Kumano Nachi Taisha – Fusumi-no-Mikoto (Senju Kannon)

Along the trail, you will also see statues of **Jizo** 地蔵, a Bodhisattva (one who delays enlightenment out

Ema votive tablets: people buy these, write their wishes on them and hang them in the shrine grounds

of compassion for mankind) who has long been considered the guardian of children, firemen and travellers. Jizo statues are often placed on pilgrimage trails to protect pilgrims, and also in cemeteries or temples (often with a red bib) for parents to pray for the souls of their deceased children. The three-legged **Yatagarasu** 八咫烏 crow of Japan's creation myth is depicted at each of the three grand shrines;

its feet are said to represent heaven, earth and mankind. Each of the three grand shrines has a unique image of the Yatagarasu and it is also used as the logo for the Japan Football Association.

THE PILGRIMAGE TRAILS

The Kumano Kodo is made up of five pilgrimage trails: the Kiiji, Nakahechi, Ohechi, Kohechi and Iseji, which lead

GLOSSARY OF RELIGIOUS TERMS

Shugendo 修験道: a religion combining ancient mountain worship, Shintoism, Esoteric Buddhism and Taoism, established in the seventh century by En no Gyoja. Priests who practise Shugendo are called **Yamabushi**.

Shrines and stupas
Jinja 神社: a Shinto shrine

Oji 王子: a subsidiary or child shrine of the Kumano Sanzan, thought to have been erected by Shugendo priests to provide a place of rest, purification and worship. They were often referred to as the 99-*oji* as there were so many, and there were five main *oji* called **gotai-oji**: Fujishiro-oji, Kirime-oji, Inabane-oji, Takijiri-oji, and Hosshinmon-oji.

Shimenawa 標縄: a rope that is hung, often on *torii* gates and in shrines, or tied around objects (trees, rocks, etc), denoting the boundary of the secular and the sacred

Stupa 塔: Buddhist monuments (based on ancient mounds from India) used to contain sutras and relics and later used as tombstones. **Gorintou** 五輪塔 are five-tiered stupas representing earth, water, fire, wind and space.

Taisha 大社: grand shrine

Temizuya 手水舎: water purification basin at the entrance to shrines and temples

Torii 鳥居: 'bird perch' – *torii* gates are associated with Shinto and mark the boundary between the secular and sacred worlds

Talismans and tokens
Ema 絵馬: meaning 'picture horse', these are wooden tablets traditionally depicting a horse but nowadays it depends on the shrine – the Kumano

Sanzan shrines all depict a Yatagarasu crow. People buy the tablets, write their wishes and hang them in the grounds.

Kumano Go-o-hoin 牛王宝印: paper talismans depicting the sacred Yatagarasu crow, available from each shrine. Traditionally used as a binding contract and thought to bring good luck, they are often hung above the entrance to people's homes.

Omamori お守り: protective amulet/lucky charm available from shrines

Omikuji おみくじ: white fortune slip from shrines. People tie 'bad fortunes' to a wall or tree in the shrine grounds and keep the good fortunes.

Rituals and beliefs

Koshin 庚申: Koshin originates from an ancient Taoist belief that certain days or years bring misfortune – in particular every 60th day of the Chinese sexagenary cycle. On this 'Koshin' day, people would hold a vigil to stay awake all night, believing that if you slept, the 'three worms' that live inside your body would escape and report your wrongdoings to a god who would reduce your lifespan as punishment. Koshin statues are often depicted by a tantric deity with multiple arms on top of three monkeys – see/hear/speak no evil.

Misogi 禊: water purification ritual

Nembutsu 念仏: a Buddhist prayer to invoke Amida Buddha by chanting 'Namu Amida Butsu' 南無阿弥陀仏 ('I take refuge in Amida Buddha')

Sutra: Buddhist scriptures

to the three grand shrines of Kumano. There is also a trail to Hongu called the Omine Okugakemichi, and the Choishimichi is a 1200+ year-old pilgrimage trail to Koyasan. Sections of all of these routes are designated World Heritage, with the exception of the Kiiji. These routes are described in more detail below.

Nakahechi 中辺路

The Nakahechi was the chosen route of retired emperors and became known as the Imperial Route. The Nakahechi branches off from the old Kiiji route in Tanabe and heads east through the mountains to the first of the three grand shrines, Kumano Hongu Taisha. From here, retired emperors and nobles would sail down the Kumano-gawa River to visit the next grand shrine, Kumano Hayatama Taisha in Shingu. They would then follow the coast west to the Nachi-gawa River and follow this upstream to the last of the three grand shrines, Kumano Nachi Taisha. From here they would begin the difficult journey back to Hongu and onto Kyoto, with round-trip pilgrimages usually taking a month a more.

Today, this route remains the most popular and is well waymarked with bilingual signs and excellent facilities. If you have limited time and

Ancient stone steps leading down to Nachi Falls (Kumano Nachi Taisha)

would like to experience the Kumano Kodo, then this is the trail to hike. The official starting point is beside Takijiri-oji, which is a 40min bus ride from Kii-Tanabe station. From Takijiri-oji it's a two-day hike to Hongu to visit Kumano Hongu Taisha. The river pilgrimage that retired emperors once took to visit the second grand shrine, Kumano Hayatama Taisha in Shingu, is included in the World Heritage designation and is still possible today on traditional wooden boats (the departure point is further downstream nowadays because of the upstream damming). Most pilgrims walk south-southeast from the Hongu area to Nachisan (Mt Nachi) to visit Kumano Nachi Taisha; a two-day hike with a night midway in Koguchi. From Nachisan there is bus transport down the mountain to the coastal area of Nachi-Katsuura from where you can take the train to Tanabe/Osaka or northeast towards Shingu/Ise/Nagoya.

The transport and accommodation options in this area allow you to pick and choose sections depending on time, fitness and budget. The waymarking also allows you to walk in either direction. Recommended stages are:

1. Takijiri-oji to Tsugizakura-oji, 16.4km
2. Tsugizakura-oji to Kumano Hongu Taisha, 20.6km
3. Rest day – take the traditional boat tour along the Kumano-gawa River in the morning to visit Kumano Hayatama Taisha in Shingu, then return to Hongu by bus in the afternoon

A grazing pony in the yard of Coffee Keyaki, Takahara (Nakahechi, Stage 1)

4   Hongu (Ukegawa) to Koguchi (this trail is called the Kogumotori-goe), 12.6km
5   Koguchi to Kumano Nachi Taisha (this trail is called the Ogumotori-goe), 14.2km

Hongu loop

There is also the Hongu loop walk for those with limited time. The whole loop is 16.7km but can be broken into three stages. The last 7km from Hosshinmon-oji is particularly popular.

Kohechi 小辺路

This 63km route was developed as the shortest way over the mountains down the middle of the Kii Peninsula from Koyasan's Shingon Buddhist Complex to Hongu. The first account of a pilgrim walking this route dates to 1573: a military commander named Doi Kiyoyoshi from Iyo Province (present-day Ehime in Shikoku) walked from Koyasan to visit the Kumano Sanzan and then continued along the Iseji route to Ise, in honour of his father who had recently died in battle.

The Kohechi is a challenging, isolated and often steep mountainous route, involving daily mountain passes over 1000m high. Certain sections of the trail (namely the two middle mountains, Obako-toge and Miura-toge) are subject to landslides. This trail is recommended for fit and experienced hikers, from April to October. There is very limited public transportation, basic services and minimal accommodation (often the only source of meals) which should be booked well in advance to guarantee a bed. At the time of writing (spring 2018), the trail was mostly waymarked with bilingual signs. Mountain notification boxes 登山届 – boxes containing forms that should be completed with your contact details, hiking plan and emergency contact information – are placed at each trailhead, or details can be submitted online at www.police.pref.nara.jp/cmsform/enquete.php?id=16

Recommended stages are:

1 Koyasan to Omata, 16.8km
2 Omata to Miura-guchi, 14km
3 Miura-guchi to Totsukawa Onsen, 18.3km
4 Totsukawa Onsen to Hongu, 14.3km

If you have limited time, it's possible to just walk the last stage over Hatenashi-toge Pass from Totsukawa Onsen to Hongu (or vice versa), as there is a good bus service between these two areas. The bus schedule can be downloaded from the Tanabe tourism website, www.tb-kumano.jp/en (select 'Transport', 'Bus', then 'Timetables' and look for the Gojo – Shingu line).

Iseji 伊勢路

This 170km trail links Japan's most sacred Shinto shrine (Ise-jingu, dedicated to the sun goddess Amaterasu, mythical ancestor of the emperor) with the Kumano Sanzan along the southeast coast of the Kii Peninsula. The route was once popular with people coming from the north as well as pilgrims walking the 33 Kannon pilgrimage; Seiganto-ji Temple at Mt Nachi is the first of the 33 temples. There was even a popular saying, 'Seven times to

Descending along ishitatami flagstone from Magose-toge Pass (Iseji)

Ise, three times to Kumano.' The most revered site along the route, other than Ise-jingu Shrine, is Hana-no-Iwaya in Kumano City (see Iseji highlights – Matsumoto-toge Pass) which, according to Japan's creation myth, is believed to be the grave of Izanami-no-Mikoto, goddess creator of Japan.

Two 'highlight' routes have been included in this guide. Walking the full length of the Iseji route is a real adventure and feels like stepping back in time to the Edo period, with many of the villages resembling samurai film sets! There are currently no waymarks in English or Japanese other than on the mountain passes, however, Mie Prefecture has produced an online navigational GPS for phones (you'll need a battery power backup if following this for 7+ hours a day). This and other information in English can be found at www.kodo.pref.mie.lg.jp/en. The author of this guide has high hopes for a full Iseji route guide in the future.

Koyasan – Choishimichi (stone marker path) 高野山 町石道

This 20km trail was constructed by Kobo Daishi in the ninth century from the valley floor up to the high mountain basin of Koyasan, where he established the headquarters of his Shingon Buddhism school. Emperors, feudal lords, monks and pilgrims have been walking this route for more than 1200 years. The original 180 wooden stupas placed along the trail at intervals of one *cho* (about 109m) were replaced in the 13th century with Gorinto-shaped stone markers representing the five elements of earth, water, fire, wind and space. The name Choishimichi is made up of three words: *cho* (a measurement of distance), *ishi* (stone) and *michi* (path/road). Today the path is waymarked with bilingual signs from Jison-in Temple to Daimon gate and is an enjoyable alternative to catching the train, cable car and bus to the top. Walking down might be even more enjoyable!

Other trails not included in this guide

Kiiji 紀伊路

This was the route from the ancient capital of Kyoto, originally followed by retired emperors who travelled by boat along the Yodo-gawa River to Kubotsu-oji (the first of the 99-*oji*) in Osaka. They then travelled overland to Tanabe where the route split into two, forming the Nakahechi and Ohechi trails. Little remains of this path today.

Ohechi 大辺路

This 120km trail from Tanabe followed the coast around to Nachi-Katsuura before merging with the Nakahechi and following the Nachi-gawa River upstream to Kumano Nachi Taisha. The route offered stunning views of the Pacific Ocean and was popular with poets and artists. Today there are just a few mountain-pass sections preserved (Tonda-zaka

---

DON'T MISS

- The three grand shrines of Kumano: Kumano Hongu Taisha, Kumano Hayatama Taisha and Kumano Nachi Taisha
- Visiting Koyasan, staying in a Buddhist temple and eating *shojin-ryori* (Buddhist vegetarian cuisine)
- Bathing in Tsuboyu, the only UNESCO World Heritage-listed *onsen* (hot spring) in the world (in Yunomine Onsen)
- Traditional boat tour down the Kumano-gawa River to Kumano Hayatama Taisha in Shingu
- Climbing the 538 steps to Kamikura-jinja Shrine and Gotobiki-iwa rock with a view of Shingu and the Pacific Ocean

Nakahechi route
- The view of Hongu from Fushiogami-oji (Stage 2)
- The view of Hongu's O-torii from the side-trail between Nakahechi waymarks 73 and 74 (Stage 2)
- Views of the Hyakken-gura sea of mountains (Stage 3)
- Views of the Pacific Ocean from the Funami-chaya teahouse remains (Stage 4)

Kohechi route
- 360-degree views from Obako-toge summit (Stage 2)
- Hatenashi Settlement (Stage 4)

Iseji route
- Iseji highlights – both routes feature traditional *ishitatami* flagstone paths and have fantastic views

---

and Nagai-zaka, for example) but unfortunately the route largely involves dangerous road-walking along Route 42.

Omine Okugakemichi 大峯奥駈道
This is the name of the trail linking Yoshino and Omine in Nara Prefecture to the Kumano Sanzan. Characterised by steep and rugged mountain trails up to 2000m, it was historically used as a training ground

for Yamabushi mountain ascetics practising Shugendo (a fusion of Shinto, Buddhism and Taoism), and is believed to have been founded by En no Gyoja in the seventh century.

DUAL PILGRIM STATUS

The Kumano Kodo in Japan and the Camino de Santiago in Spain are the only two UNESCO World Heritage-listed pilgrimages in the world, and as

Dual Pilgrim certificate, credential and stamps

such they have been 'twinned'. Hikers who complete the following are eligible to register as a Dual Pilgrim:

* **Camino de Santiago:** walk at least the last 100km or cycle at least the last 200km, collecting stamps in a pilgrim credential
  and
* **Kumano Kodo:** walk at least one of the following four options, collecting stamps in the Dual Pilgrim credential along the way:
  * Nakahechi route – Takijiri-oji to Kumano Hongu Taisha (37km)
  * Nakahechi route – Kumano Hongu Taisha to Kumano Nachi Taisha (27km)
  * Nakahechi route – Hosshinmon-oji to Kumano

Hongu Taisha (7km), plus a stamp from Kumano Hayatama Taisha and Kumano Nachi Taisha
  * Kohechi route – Koyasan to Kumano Hongu Taisha (63km)

Dual Pilgrim credentials (a booklet used to collect stamps, including the list of stamps required) and completion stamps are available in:

Spain

* Santiago de Compostela Tourist Office (Rúa do Vilar, 63, www.santiagoturismo.com, open May–Oct daily 9am–9pm, Nov–Apr Mon–Fri 9am–7pm, weekends and holidays 9am–2pm and 4–7pm)

Japan

* Tanabe Tourist Information Center, next to Kii-Tanabe station

27

(www.tb-kumano.jp/en, open Mon–Fri 9am–5pm)

- Kumano Hongu Heritage Center, opposite the entrance to Kumano Hongu Taisha (www.city.tanabe. lg.jp/hongukan/en, open daily 8.30am–5pm)
- Kumano Kodo Kan Pilgrimage Center opposite Takijiri-oji (www. tb-kumano.jp/en – see 'Area Guide' – open daily 9am–5pm)

A completion certificate is also available at the Tanabe Tourist Information Center or Kumano Hongu Heritage Center; you can also opt in to be featured on the Dual Pilgrim Spiritual Pilgrimages website: http:// dual-pilgrim.spiritual-pilgrimages. com

Dual Pilgrim stamps スタンプ can be collected at the three grand shrines and along the Nakahechi and Kohechi trails (stamp lists are available with the credentials). The charming red ink stamps – depicting various scenes including shrines, teahouses, waterfalls and Jizo statues – are a joy to find and leave you with a lovely memento of your pilgrimage.

WILDLIFE

There are a few creatures to be aware of while hiking in this region, including the Japanese giant hornet, the giant centipede, venomous snakes (the Japanese pit viper and tiger keelback), bears and wild boar. For further details, see 'Staying healthy and safe' below.

In addition to the 'not-so-safe' wildlife, you might also encounter the following:

Birds

The **Black-eared kite** (*tobi*), *Milvus lineatus*, is abundant in Japan and is known to swoop down and snatch food, so be warned! Other birds you're more likely to hear than see include the **Japanese pygmy woodpecker** (*kogera*), *Yungipicus kizuki*, and the beautiful sound of the **Japanese bush warbler** (*uguisu*), *Horornis diphone*.

Reptiles

Common non-venomous snakes you may encounter include:

- **Japanese rat snake** (*aodaisho*), *Elaphe climacophora*, which grows up to 2m long. Colouration varies from yellow/brown to olive-green and it has dark blotches along the body.
- **Japanese four-lined rat snake** (*shimahebi*), *Elaphe quadrivirgata* – smaller than the above rat snake, this is easily identifiable by the four dark lines along its body. It's also possible to see black versions of this snake, called *karasu hebi*.

The most common lizards are the **Japanese grass lizard** (*kanahebi*), *Takydromus tachydromoides*, and **Japanese five-lined skink** (*nihon tokage*), *Plestiodon japonicas* – the juveniles and females have a distinctive bright blue tail.

Mammals

Japanese macaque (*saru*), *Macaca fuscata*, are located all over Japan. These cheeky monkeys with red faces and red bottoms also inhabit the forests of the Kii Peninsula, though you'll be lucky to see one. You may spot **Sika deer** (*shika*), *Cervus nippon*, and if you're really lucky you might see a **raccoon-dog** (*tanuki*), *Nyctereutes procyonoides* – about the size of a fox but with raccoon-like markings. *Tanuki* are a much-loved part of Japanese culture and are considered to be mischievous creatures with shape-shifting powers (watch the Japanese anime *Pom Poko*). They're also believed to bring prosperity, so statues of *tanuki* can be found outside many bars and restaurants, often depicted with a big belly, large testicles and holding a bottle of sake!

Other

Japanese freshwater crabs (*sawagani*), *Geothelphusa dehaani*, are easily spotted with their orange/red backs as they scuttle over the trails near streams. **Frogs** (*kaeru*), **toads** (*hikigaeru*) and **newts** (*imori*) like the **Japanese fire belly newt**, *Cynops pyrrhogaster* – which is black with a red underside – are also common after wet weather and near streams. There are also numerous **butterflies** (*chocho*) and **dragonflies** (*tonbo*).

GROUP TRAVEL OR INDEPENDENT?

At first glance, the number of pilgrimage trails and various options may seem daunting, but your options really break down into the Nakahechi (the most popular route, 1–4 days), Kohechi (a challenging mountainous route for experienced hikers, 1 or 4 days), Koyasan trail (1 day) and Iseji highlights (1–2 days). If you have limited time and sufficient budget, consider a guided or self-guided tour with all your accommodation, meals,

Kumano Hongu Heritage Center, Hongu

bag transfers and transport arranged. If booking independently, check out the excellent Kumano Travel www.kumano-travel.com/en (run by the Tanabe Tourist Information Center); you can book your whole trip online from accommodation to luggage transfers and optional tours, and there are a number of suggested itineraries on the website. If hiking in the peak seasons of spring or autumn, make sure to book well in advance. While telephone numbers are mostly provided for accommodation (for emergency purposes only), English is not commonly spoken. It is strongly advisable to make bookings online or through an agency unless you are fluent in Japanese.

Guided and self-guided tours

For a list of organisations offering guided and self-guided tours of the Kumano Kodo, see Appendix C.

Budgeting

If you book a guided or self-guided tour then you'll be paying the bulk of the costs upfront and will have little to pay on the ground (lunches, bus rides, souvenirs). If booking independently, budget for the following daily costs per person:

- Accommodation including dinner and breakfast: ¥8000–12,000+ per night
- A lunchbox provided by your accommodation: ¥500–750

- Incidentals like bus rides, snacks, vending machine drinks: ¥500–1500

Giving an overall cost of around ¥9000–14,250 (£60–100/€70–110/US$80–130) per person per day.

GETTING THERE

Visas

British, Australian, Canadian, EU and US citizens do not require a visa for stays of up to 90 days, although you may need to provide evidence of onward travel (eg a return ticket). Citizens of other countries, or those wishing to stay longer than 90 days or intending to work or study in Japan, should check with the Japanese embassy or consulate for your country prior to travel.

Flights and onward travel

All of the hiking trails described in this guide are located on the Kii Peninsula, which is in the Kansai region due south of Kyoto. Flying from abroad, Osaka's Kansai International Airport (KIX) is the closest and most convenient airport, but with a fabulous transport system and the chance to see Mt Fuji from the bullet train, flying into Tokyo's Narita (NRT) or Haneda (HND) airports are also an option. The closest domestic airport to Tanabe (the traditional starting point of the Nakahechi route) is Nanki Shirahama Airport (SHM) in Shirahama. For train timetables in English, see

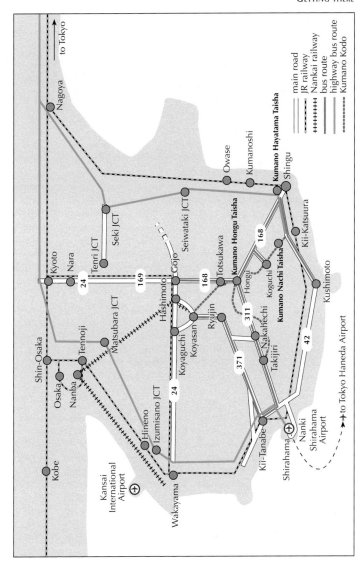

www.hyperdia.com; for train travel information and route maps in English, see www.westjr.co.jp/global/en

From the UK it's possible to fly direct to Osaka (British Airways) and Tokyo (British Airways/Japan Airlines/ANA). There aren't any low-budget flights from the UK to Japan. If flying from Australia, Jetstar is a low-budget airline that flies to Osaka's Kansai International Airport. Price comparison sites such as Skyscanner, www.skyscanner.net, may be useful in searching for and booking flights. See also Appendix C for transport contact details.

Arriving in Osaka – Kansai International Airport
Airport code: KIX, www.kansai-airport.or.jp/en

To Tanabe 田辺, Wakayama Prefecture by train
1   Kansai International Airport 関西空港 to Hineno 日根野 (JR Kansai airport line 関西空港線, 10min)
2   Hineno 日根野 to Kii-Tanabe 紀伊田辺 (JR Kinokuni line きのくに線, 1hr 35min (express train))
Note that although the city is called Tanabe 田辺, the station is called Kii-Tanabe 紀伊田辺, not to be confused with Tanabe station in Osaka.

To Mt Koya (Koyasan) 高野山 by train, cable car and bus
1   Kansai International Airport 関西空港 to Tengachaya 天下茶屋 (Nankai line 南海電気鉄道, 35min)
2   Tengachaya 天下茶屋 to Hashimoto 橋本 (Wakayama Prefecture), (Nankai Koya line 南海高野線, 45min)
3   Hashimoto 橋本 to Gokurakubashi 極楽橋 (Nankai Koya line 南海高野線, 40min)
4   Gokurakubashi 極楽橋 to Koyasan 高野山 (Nankai Koyasan cable car 南海 高野山ケーブル, 5min)
5   You've now arrived on top of the mountain but there is no pedestrian access from the station to the centre of town so you must take a bus. The bus station is adjacent and is timed to coincide with the cable car. For the centre of town, get off at Senjuinbashi east bus stop (bus stop no. 6, 10min) 千手院橋 (東) which is in front of the central tourist office. See http://eng.shukubo.net/sightseeing-place.html for a detailed map of Koyasan including temple accommodation and bus stops.

To Mt Koya (Koyasan) 高野山 by limousine bus
Kansai Airport Transportation Enterprise (www.kate.co.jp/en) operates a seasonal bus service from Kansai International Airport to Koyasan. The journey takes 1hr 45min and costs around ¥2000. For the schedule and to book online (recommended), see www.willerexpress.com. There are two drop-off points in Koyasan:

Okunoin-mae 奥の院前, which is in front of Okunoin at the east end of town, and Daimon south parking lot 大門南駐車場 which is a short walk from Daimon gate, west of town.

Arriving in Tokyo – Narita International Airport

(Located in Chiba Prefecture, 60km outside of Tokyo)

Airport code: NRT, www.narita-airport.jp/en

To Shin Osaka by train

1　Narita International Airport 成田空港 to Tokyo 東京 (JR Narita Express 成田エクスプレス, 60min)

Early-morning sun shining through the trees on the Nakahechi route, Stage 3

2　Tokyo 東京 to Shin Osaka 新大阪 (bullet train 新幹線, 2hr 30min–3hr)

(From Narita airport it's also possible – and often much cheaper than the bullet train – to fly to Kansai International Airport, then continue onto Tanabe or Koyasan. See 'Arriving in Osaka' for details.)

Arriving in Tokyo – Haneda Airport

(Located a 20min train journey from central Tokyo)

Airport code: HND, www.haneda-airport.jp/en

To Shin Osaka 新大阪 by train

1　Haneda Airport 羽田空港 to Shinagawa 品川 (Keikyu line 京浜急行電鉄, 20min)
2　Shinagawa 品川 to Shin Osaka 新大阪 (bullet train 新幹線, 2hr 30min–3hr)

(From Haneda airport it's also possible to fly to Kansai International Airport or Nanki Shirahama Airport, then continue onto Tanabe or Koyasan. See 'Arriving in Osaka' below for details.)

Shin Osaka 新大阪 to Tanabe by train

There are express trains (2hr 15min) on the JR Kinokuni line きのくに線. Note that although the city is called Tanabe 田辺, the station is called Kii-Tanabe 紀伊田辺, not to be confused with Tanabe station in Osaka.

Shin Osaka 新大阪 to Mt Koya 高野山 (Koyasan) by train, cable car and bus

1   Shin Osaka 新大阪 to Osaka 大阪 (various JR lines, 4min)
2   Osaka 大阪 to Shinimamiya 新今宮 (Osaka loop line 大阪環状線, 13min)
3   Shinimamiya 新今宮 to Hashimoto 橋本 (Nankai Koya line 南海高野線, 48min)
4   Hashimoto 橋本 to Gokurakubashi 極楽橋 (Nankai Koya line 南海高野線, 40min)
5   Gokurakubashi 極楽橋 to Koyasan 高野山 (Nankai Koyasan cable car 南海 高野山ケーブル, 5min)
6   You've now arrived on top of the mountain but there is no pedestrian access from the station to the centre of town so you must take a bus. The bus station is adjacent and is timed to coincide with the cable car. For the centre of town, get off at Senjuinbashi east bus stop (bus stop no. 6, 10min) 千手院橋 (東) which is in front of the central tourist office. See http://eng.shukubo.net/sightseeing-place.html for a detailed map of Koyasan including temple accommodation and bus stops.

Domestic flights to Nanki Shirahama

(Located in Shirahama on the Kii Peninsula only 15km south of Tanabe) Airport code: SHM, www.shirahama-airport.jp

To Tanabe by bus and train

1   Nanki Shirahama Airport 南紀白浜空港 to Shirahama train station 白浜駅 (bus, 20min)*
2   Shirahama train station 白浜駅 to Kii-Tanabe 紀伊田辺 (JR Kinokuni line きのくに線, 15min)

*Depending on the schedule, you may be able to get a bus all the way from Nanki Shirahama Airport to Tanabe (40min).

Between Koyasan and Kumano Hongu Taisha

There are two daily buses (morning and afternoon) operating from April to November – this service is called the 'Koyasan and Kumano Access Bus'. The journey takes 4hr–4hr 30min from Koyasan station to Hongu-taisha-mae bus stop (in front of Kumano Hongu Taisha) and costs around ¥5000. For more information and to book, see http://japanbusonline.com/en

GETTING AROUND

Bus timetables servicing the Nakahechi route (including Tanabe, Hongu, Shingu, Nachisan) and Totsukawa Onsen can be downloaded from the Tanabe Tourist Information Center website: www.tb-kumano.jp/en. Links for local timetables, where available, are provided in the route descriptions.

Riding local buses

1   Get on the bus (usually at the back unless there is only one door) and

Colourful plantlife on the Kumano Kodo

take a numbered ticket (*sei-ri-ken* 整理券) from the machine next to the door.

2 Push the buzzer when you hear your stop announced.

3 Check the number of your ticket on the electronic display at the front of the bus and the corresponding fare will be displayed under the ticket number.

4 Put the exact change and your numbered ticket into the machine next to the bus driver and get off. (If you don't have the exact money, you can change ¥1000 notes in the machine.)

Riding local trains

1 Buy a ticket at the station* for your destination and use this to enter through the barrier, then hold onto your ticket.

2 Get off the train at your destination and use the ticket to exit through the barrier.

*If there is no ticket office or entrance barrier at the station, board the train and take a numbered ticket (*sei-ri-ken* 整理券) from the machine next to the door. When you arrive at your destination, show the conductor your numbered ticket and pay the required amount.

Taxis

Taxi stands are often outside train stations but if you're planning to use a taxi for a longer journey, check the price beforehand (taking a bus might be a better option).

Bicycle

Many places rent bicycles by the hour or half-day, including tourist offices in Koyasan, Tanabe, Hongu, Shingu, and Nachi-Katsuura.

Coin lockers

Coin lockers of varying sizes can be found at most train stations and take ¥100 coins. Prices usually range from ¥300 to ¥500. Vending machines are usually found nearby if you need change (by buying a drink; they accept ¥1000 notes).

WHEN TO GO

Although it has a generally mild climate, the southern Kii Peninsula has one of the highest annual rainfalls in Japan, receiving an average rainfall of around 4000mm a year – so consider yourself lucky if you stay dry for your entire trip! Typically, the driest months are in winter from November to February and the wettest from June to October. Koyasan is

Spring foliage on Stage 2 of the Nakahechi route

at an elevation of 815m, compared to Tanabe at 7m or Hongu at 60m, and is consequently colder with high snowfall from December to March. For detailed weather information, see the Japan Meteorological Agency (English-language option available) www.jma.go.jp or Japan National Tourism Organization www.jnto.go.jp/weather/eng

Spring (March–May) – a wonderful time to visit with daily highs from around 15°C in March to 25°C in May. Spring is also the peak season and a chance to see cherry blossoms, magnolias, azaleas and a number of wildflowers, as well as hearing the constant chorus of the *uguisu* (Japanese bush warbler). For blossom forecasts see www.japan-guide.com/sakura

Rainy season (mid June–mid July) – hot, humid and rainy days. Excessive rain makes the flagstone paths slippery.

Summer (June–August) – daily highs from around 27°C in June to 33°C in August with high humidity. Summer is probably the least comfortable time to be hiking in this region (unless at higher elevations like on the Kohechi), but there are many summer festivals at this time.

Typhoon season (May–October, with the majority arriving in August and September) – typhoons (台風) usually develop in the south around Okinawa and travel northeast through Honshu bringing strong winds, high tides and heavy rain which can result in landslides and flooding in coastal and mountainous areas.

Autumn (September–November) – along with spring, late autumn is another ideal time to visit, with daily highs starting to decrease and average highs ranging from 28°C in September to 17°C in November. Autumn maple foliage can be seen in Koyasan and some parts of the Kumano Kodo. For maple forecasts see www.japan-guide.com (under 'Interests', select 'See All Interests', 'Autumn Colors' and 'Best Timing'.)

Winter (December–February) – the Kohechi is deemed closed in winter (except for Hatenashi-toge Pass) due to high snowfall, and snow is also to be expected along the Choishimichi trail and in Koyasan. The Nakahechi is considered open year-round, but some accommodation may be closed during winter so check in advance and take adequate rain gear and warm-weather clothing. Average daily highs range from 12°C in December to 10°C in January/February.

Holidays and festivals

During peak times like spring and Golden Week (the cluster of public holidays in late April/early May), accommodation in the small villages and in Koyasan may book out months in advance. However, if hiking the Nakahechi there are a number of places to stay in the spa resorts of Yunomine, Wataze and Kawayu Onsen, as well as in Tanabe or Hongu, so you could base yourself in these areas and use buses to get to and from the trailhead. During holidays

The annual spring festival of Kumano Hongu Taisha with Oyunohara's O-torii gate in the background

and festivals, expect public transport to be crowded; come with plenty of patience if travelling during peak periods. That being said, if you're there for the last day of the Kumano Hongu Taisha annual spring festival (15 April), or any of the numerous Koyasan festivals, you won't be disappointed.

Month	Day	Name	Area
January	1	New Year's Day	National holiday
	second Monday	Coming of Age Day	National holiday
	8	Yunomine Yoka Yakushi festival	Toko-ji Temple, Yunomine Onsen
	12	Kawayu Jyuni Yakushi festival	Kawayu Onsen
February	1–5	Ya Ya Matsuri (quarrelling festival)	Owase
	2	Hana no Iwaya-jinja Shrine Spring festival	Kumano City
	3	Setsubun Matsuri (bean-throwing festival)	National festival
	6	Oto Matsuri (fire festival)	Shingu

Month	Day	Name	Area
February	11	**National Foundation Day**	**National holiday**
March	first Sunday	Hi Matsuri (fire ceremony)	Koyasan
	3	Hina Matsuri (doll festival)	National festival
	20/21	**Vernal Equinox Day**	**National holiday**
April	8	Hana Matsuri (Buddha's birthday)	National festival
	13–15	Kumano Hongu Taisha Festival	Hongu
	third Sunday	Hanamori Matsuri (spring flowers festival)	Niutsuhime-jinja Shrine, Choishimichi route
	29	**Showa Day**	**National holiday**
	end April/ beginning May	Golden Week	National festival
May	end April/ beginning May	Golden Week	National festival
	3	**Constitution Memorial Day**	**National holiday**
	3–5	Spring Kechien Kanjo ceremony	Koyasan
	4–5	Sanada festival	Kudoyama (Choishimichi)
	4	**Greenery Day**	**National holiday**
	5	**Children's Day**	**National holiday**
	5	Funatama-jinja Shrine festival	Nakahechi route
June	15	Aoba Matsuri (Kobo Daishi's birthday festival)	Koyasan
July	7	Tanabata Matsuri (star festival)	National festival
	14	Nachi-no-hi Matsuri (Kumano Nachi Taisha fire festival)	Nachisan
	14	Ogitate Matsuri (fan festival)	Kumano Hayatama Taisha
	third Monday	**Marine Day**	**National holiday**
	24–25	Tanabe Matsuri (Tanabe festival)	Tanabe
August	11	**Mountain Day**	**National holiday**

Month	Day	Name	Area
August	mid	Bon festival	National festival
	13	Rosoku Matsuri (candle festival)	Koyasan
	mid	Kumano fireworks festival	Shichiri-mihama Coast, Kumano City
	last Saturday	Yata-no-hi Matsuri (Yata fire festival)	Hongu
September	**third Monday**	**Respect for the Aged Day**	**National holiday**
	22/23	**Autumnal Equinox Day**	**National holiday**
October	1–3	Autumn Kechien Kanjo ceremony	Koyasan
	first weekend	Benkei festival	Ogigahama beach, Tanabe
	15–16	Kumano Hayatama Taisha annual festival	Shingu
	16	Mifune Matsuri (Mifune boat festival)	Kumano-gawa River
	second Monday	**Health and Sports Day**	**National holiday**
November	**3**	**Culture Day**	**National holiday**
	3	Kumano Kodo pilgrimage procession	Takahara
	15	Shichi-go-san festival	National festival
	23	**Labor Thanksgiving Day**	**National holiday**
December	1 Dec–28 Feb	Sennin-buro outside bath in Kawayu River is open	Kawayu Onsen
	23	**Emperor's Birthday**	**National holiday**

For a list of nationwide festivals, see www.jnto.go.jp/eng/pdf (select 'Special interests' on the left, then 'Annual Events in Japan'). For a list of festivals in the Tanabe area, see www.tb-kumano.jp/en (select 'What to do', then 'Festivals & Events' on the right). For a list of festivals in Koyasan, see http://eng.shukubo.net ('Events Calendar').

ACCOMMODATION

Staying in a traditional Japanese inn along any of the Kumano Kodo trails will be a highlight of your trip,

Traditional Japanese room at Shizen-no-Ie, Koguchi (Nakahechi, Stage 3)

but accommodation is limited and advanced reservations are necessary in order to secure a bed and meals.

If booking accommodation independently, the best way for most of the trails described in this guide is through the local Tanabe Tourism agency, Kumano Travel www.kumano-travel.com/en. There are also a number of options available through www.booking.com, www.airbnb.com, www.japaneseguesthouses.com and Koyasan's temple lodging website http://eng.shukubo.net. Unless you are fluent in Japanese it is best to book online or through an agency, as English is not commonly spoken by the accommodation providers.

Washitsu 和室 means Japanese-style and refers to a bedroom with tatami (mats made from rice straw) and futons that are laid out each night, then packed away in the morning. Shoes are taken off at the entrance and exchanged for 'inside slippers'. The inside slippers are then removed at the entrance to your room if it has tatami flooring. Yukata (dressing gowns) are usually provided for you to wear around the establishment, to dinner and bed. Rooms may have a private WC but bathrooms are typically communal, segregated by sex – see 'Cultural etiquette' for more information on Japanese baths.

Youshitsu 洋室 means Western-style.

Prices in this guide are starting rates and are per person (pp) unless otherwise specified. (Most accommodation in Japan is priced per person except for rental houses and hotels.) The following key is used throughout the guide:

> ¥ = up to ¥4000pp
> ¥¥ = ¥4000–8000pp
> ¥¥¥ = ¥8000–12,000pp
> ¥¥¥¥ = ¥12,000–16,000pp
> ¥¥¥¥¥ = over ¥16,000pp
> D&B = dinner and breakfast
> Rooms are Japanese-style unless otherwise specified.

Minshuku 民宿

Often family-run B&B Japanese-style accommodation with futons that you may be required to lay out yourself. Bathrooms are communal, and meals (if included) will usually be served in a dining room. Prices are typically per person, starting from around ¥7000 including dinner and breakfast.

Pension ペンション

Adapted from the European style of pensions, these are often family-run B&Bs with Western-style rooms. Bathrooms are often communal, and meals (if served) may be Western-style. Prices are typically per person, starting from around ¥7000 including dinner and breakfast.

Ryokan 旅館

A Japanese-style inn with futons that are laid out for you after dinner and packed away in the morning after breakfast. Bathrooms are often communal although some rooms may have a private WC. Dinner and breakfast are often provided in your room. Prices are typically per person, starting from around ¥8000 including dinner and breakfast.

Ryokan Adumaya, Yunomine Onsen (Hongu loop)

Rental house レンタルハウス

Along the Nakahechi trail there are a few options to rent out houses. It is possible to rent these for a single night, and in some cases you may be able to arrange meals to be brought to the house or you can cook your own. Prices vary, starting from around ¥6000 per person.

Business hotels ビジネスホテル

Usually multi-floored concrete buildings conveniently situated near train stations with simple Western- or Japanese-style rooms and en-suite bathrooms. Many have coin laundry facilities and vending machines. Breakfast may be an optional extra. Prices are typically per room, starting from around ¥5000 (excluding meals).

Koyasan Shukubo temple lodging 宿坊

Of the 117 temples in Koyasan, 52 offer accommodation, with varying price structures based on room type (garden-facing, for example) and meals. Shojin-Ryori Buddhist vegetarian cuisine is served for dinner and breakfast, and you will often have the opportunity to participate in the temple's early-morning ceremonies, called *otsutome*. (Take earplugs if you're a light sleeper as the walls are often literally paper thin.) Prices are typically per person, starting from around ¥9000 including dinner and breakfast.

Campgrounds キャンプ場

Although few and far between and mostly geared towards car-camping, there are campgrounds in Chikatsuyu, Kawayu Onsen and Wataze Onsen. As most of the Kumano Kodo trails are within the Yoshino Kumano National Park, camping is not permitted outside of designated campgrounds.

FOOD AND DRINK

Along the Kumano Kodo routes, many of the accommodation options are in small villages and are often the only source of meals. Unless staying in a city or large town (Tanabe, Nachi-Katsuura, Shingu, Owase), opt for half-board with the option to request a lunchbox. Mealtimes in Japanese inns in these rural areas are usually fixed at around 6pm for dinner and 7.30am for breakfast. Japanese-style food is called *washoku* 和食 and Western-style is called *youshoku* 洋食.

Note that the legal drinking age in Japan is 20.

Meals

Breakfast

Western-style breakfasts often include toast with jam, yoghurt, eggs, ham/bacon and salad but can be on the light side. Japanese-style breakfasts are a much heartier affair, typically with rice, pickles, tofu, miso soup and grilled fish. Green tea and water are usually provided. Instant coffee may be available; if not, try the nearest vending machine for (hot and cold) coffee in a can (it's surprisingly good!). If buying your breakfast from a store, you'll find items like cereal, milk, bread, fruit, sweet cakes (doughnuts/hotcakes), yoghurt and juice.

Lunch

If your accommodation has prepared you a *bento* (lunchbox), it might include rice balls with various fillings (sour plum, pickles, salmon), and perhaps tempura, pickles, slices of fruit as well as a bottle of water or green tea. If buying your own lunch from a store, you'll find ready-made sandwiches as well as bread/ham/cheese, etc, to make your own, and *onigiri* (rice balls

Traditional wooden shops – Kawahara Yokocho – next to Kumano Hayatama Taisha

with various fillings), sushi, *bento* lunchboxes, fruit and chocolate bars.

Dinner

If dinner is included at your accommodation, expect an impeccably presented multi-course (*kaiseki*) dinner using seasonal and local ingredients. The staple dishes are rice, pickles, fish (raw and cooked) and soup, and other courses may include *sansai* (mountain vegetables), tempura, tofu, Kumano beef and hotpots. If staying at a Koyasan temple, the Buddhist vegetarian cuisine you'll be eating is called *shojin ryori* – see below for a description. If staying in a town or city and dinner isn't included, head to the nearest *izakaya* (a Japanese-style pub) where you'll be able to sample various dishes often including *yakitori* (grilled chicken skewers), sushi and

fried dishes. Beer (pronounced *beeru*) and local sake (*Nihonshu*, meaning Japanese alcohol) are available for purchase at most Japanese inns and some may also serve the deliciously sweet plum wine (*umeshu*). Wine and spirits are not readily available in inns but are in restaurants and *izakayas*.

Trail snacks

While items like granola/muesli bars or trail mix are hard to find in Japan, you will find dried and fresh fruit, nuts, chocolate (Snickers, M&Ms, interestingly flavoured Kit-Kats), biscuits and a variety of energy/protein bars in stores. 'CalorieMate' is a popular 'nutritionally balanced source of the energy' bar (like a shortbread biscuit); try the maple flavour.

Purchasing food

Convenience stores

Family Mart, 7–Eleven and Lawson are just a few of the convenience stores you'll see and appreciate for being open 24 hours a day. Many also have free wi-fi. You can buy basic first-aid items (plasters, bandages), toiletries, batteries, ready-made meals like pasta/curry/sushi/tempura (hot meals can be heated instore), pot noodles, snacks, fruit, drinks, alcohol and more.

Michi-no-eki

Meaning 'road station', these are a network of rest areas along highways with shops selling local produce and souvenirs. Some also have a café/restaurant as well as a WC, vending machine, payphone and rest shelter. There's a *michi-no-eki* on Nakahechi Stage 1, Kohechi Stage 4, Choishimichi and Iseji Magose-toge. See www.michino-eki.jp/stations/english

Vending machines

The abundance of vending machines, most of which are in the open air and accessible 24 hours a day, means you're never too far from a drink.

HELPFUL PHRASES

- I'm vegetarian – *Watashi wa bejitarian desu* 私はベジタリアンです or *Watashi wa saishoku shugi-sha desu* 私は菜食主義者です
- Does this contain meat or fish? – *Kore wa niku ya sakana ga haitte imasuka?* これは肉や魚が入っていますか?
- I don't eat meat or fish – *Watashi wa niku ya sakana o tabemasen* 私は肉や魚を食べません
- I don't eat (…) – *Watashi wa (…) o tabemasen* 私は (…) を食べません
- I can eat (…) – *Watashi wa (…) o taberaremasu* 私は (…) 食べられます
- meat – *niku* 肉, beef – *gyuniku* 牛肉, fish – *sakana* 魚, chicken – *toriniku* 鶏肉, pork – *butaniku* 豚肉, eggs – *tamago* 卵, cheese – *cheezu* チーズ, milk – *miruku* ミルク, dairy – *nyuseihin* 乳製品

Kumano Kodo specialities – mehari-zushi and tuna at Meharizushi Nidaime in Nachi-Katsuura

They usually sell coffee, water, sports and vitamin drinks and take ¥1000 notes in addition to coins. (Some also sell alcohol.) The colouring under the price indicates hot (red) or cold (blue). In built-up areas and at railway stations you may also see ice-cream or hot-food vending machines. Non-alcoholic drinks cost from ¥100 to ¥150 and beer/sake usually from ¥200.

Vegetarians ベジタリアン/菜食主義者
Pronounced *bejitarian* or *saishoku shugi-sha*, vegetarianism has been slow to catch on in Japan. That said, it's quite common to find vegetarian restaurants in cities and towns (there's a vegetarian café in Koyasan and a vegan one in Hongu), and if staying in a temple in Koyasan you will be served *shojin-ryori* (Buddhist

vegetarian cuisine). Most Japanese inns will try to accommodate vegetarians if given advanced notice, but you may need to remind people not to include animal products in stocks and sauces or as seasoning (such as dried fish flakes). Typical Japanese foods that are vegetarian include rice, pickles, tofu, mountain vegetables, tempura and edamame.

Specialities of the Kumano Kodo
*   *Mehari-zushi* めはりずし – large rice balls wrapped in pickled mustard leaves. The name means 'wide-eyed sushi' as the balls are so large you have to open your mouth and eyes wide!
*   *Sanma-zushi* さんまずし – rice topped with pacific saury (also known as mackerel pike)

- *Kakinoha-zushi* 柿の葉寿司 – rice balls with fish (often mackerel) and wrapped in persimmon leaves
- River fish like *ayu* 鮎 (sweetfish) and *amago* アマゴ (red-spotted masu salmon)

Local favourites
- Katsuura: *maguro* 鮪 (tuna), also written ツナ (pronounced 'tsuna')
- Nachisan: *jabara* ジャバラ, a citrus fruit similar to a yuzu (but with high acidity), found in souvenir shops as boiled sweets, juice and ice-cream flavours/toppings
- Tanabe: *ume* 梅 (apricots, but more often translated as plum) and *mikan* みかん (mandarin oranges)
- Totsukawa Onsen: *yubeshi* 十津川ゆべし, made with yuzu citrus, the pulp is removed and mixed with a paste including miso, sesame and peanuts. The paste is then placed inside the yuzu and it's hung outside to dry over the winter. It's often sold wrapped in rice-straw and served with rice and sake.

- Wakayama: Wakayama ramen 和歌山ラーメン
- Yunomine Onsen: food cooked with the *onsen* water and *onsen* coffee

Specialities of Koyasan
Shojin ryori 精進料理 is a Buddhist vegetarian cuisine, introduced from China in the sixth century, that uses seasonal ingredients and is based on the rule of five: five flavours (sweet, sour, salty, bitter and savoury), five colours (yellow, red, green, white and black) and at least five types of dishes (raw, fried, boiled, steamed, baked). While onion and garlic are considered too pungent and exciting for the senses, ginger, herbs, soy sauce, mirin and vinegar can be used, and the result is a flavoursome multi-course meal. Popular *shojin ryori* dishes in Koyasan include:
- *Koya tofu* 高野豆腐, reconstituted freeze-dried tofu resulting in a light and spongy dish
- *Goma dofu* 胡麻豆腐, a silky-smooth tofu made from roasted and ground sesame seeds – if

---

USEFUL PHRASES

In Japan, there are three phrases that will please your Japanese hosts when eating with them:
- *Ita-daki-masu* いただきます – this is said at the beginning of each meal and means thank you for the food you're about to receive
- *Gochi-sou-sama-deshita* ごちそうさまでした – this is said to the chef at the end of the meal and means thank you
- *O-ishi-katta-desu!* おいしかったです – that was delicious!

USEFUL INFORMATION

Time: GMT+9 (there is no daylight saving time in Japan)

Language: Japanese 日本語

Currency: Japanese yen 円/¥. Notes are available in ¥1000, ¥2000, ¥5000 and ¥10,000 denominations. Coins are available in ¥1, ¥5, ¥10, ¥50, ¥100 and ¥500. (The ¥5 coin is the only one without a Western numeral.) Exchange rates, summer 2018: £1 = ¥147; €1 = ¥131; US$1 = ¥112.

International dialling code: +81

Emergency number: 119 for fire (*kaji* 火事) and medical emergencies (*kyukyu* 救急), 110 for police (*keisatsu* 警察) – both free from public phones

Electrical power: 100V – the plug is a two-flat-pin type like in America (plug type A).

Drinking water: tap water is safe to drink.

Travel insurance: make sure to purchase adequate travel insurance that includes hiking and any other activities you are planning on doing.

you'd like to buy some in Koyasan, try the superb Hamadaya 濱田屋 shop; they make it using local springwater

Another local delicacy is the Miroku-ishi *manju* red bean cakes, available from the popular Miroku-ishi Kasakuni みろく石 本舗 かさ國 shop on the main street and named after the Miroku-ishi stone in Okunoin.

MONEY

Japan is a very cash-based society and you may find most accommodation will only accept cash for payment. Luckily, most post offices (Japan Post, which are abundant) have ATMs which accept most foreign-issued bank cards. Japan Post ATM opening hours are longer than post office

hours but are often closed on weekends. Seven Bank inside 7–Eleven convenience stores also accepts foreign-issued cards and these are open 24 hours a day. For more information about either of these ATM services, see www.jp-bank.japanpost.jp (select English-language option, then 'Service Information') or www.seven bank.co.jp (English-language option).

POST, PHONES AND INTERNET

Japan Post has offices even in some of the smallest villages and details are given of each throughout this guide. Opening hours vary depending on the location, but most are open at least Mon–Fri 9am–5pm and some are open for limited hours at the weekend. Look for the red post office symbol (〒) and for more information

A Jizo statue on the
Nakahechi route, Stage 4

data-based phone services such as Skype or WhatsApp.

Along the Kumano Kodo, wi-fi is not as widely available as would be expected of such a technologically advanced country and depending on the trail you're on, you may go a day or two before finding it (not all accommodation has wi-fi). Wakayama Prefecture has free wi-fi hotspots in popular areas (Kii-Tanabe station, Hongu, Shingu station and Kii-Katsuura station, for example) and most convenience stores also have free wi-fi. If you need 24-7 access to the internet then the best option would be to hire mobile wi-fi from the airport on arrival. For more information see www.kansai-airport. or.jp/en (search 'wi-fi router rental'), www.narita-airport.jp/en (select 'Shop & Dine, Services', then 'Service'), or www.haneda-airport.jp/inter/en (select 'Facilities', then 'Internet and Cell Phone Rental').

see www.post.japanpost.jp (English-language option).

Most public telephones accept ¥10 and ¥100 coins, so put aside some ¥10 coins in the event you need to make a local call. Prepaid international telephone cards can be purchased from the airport and convenience stores to be used in payphones; KDDI is one of the companies that offer this product, www.001.kddi. com/en. If your phone is on 3G or 4G you can use it in Japan but check with your mobile phone company beforehand regarding roaming charges. Phones or sim cards (for unlocked phones) can be rented at the airport on arrival, but this is a pricey option and unless you need to make a lot of phone calls it may be more useful to hire mobile wi-fi (see below) and use

LANGUAGE

Japanese is the official language of Japan and English is not commonly spoken outside of the large cities. If travelling with a smartphone, consider downloading a translation app; Google Translate, for example, allows you to download an offline translation of Japanese, meaning you can simply hover your phone camera over the text to see the translation. There are a number of pocket Japanese phrasebooks published by Lonely

Planet, Collins, Berlitz and others, as well as a basic Japanese glossary included in Appendix B in this guide. Sentence structure in Japan is different to English and follows the 'subject, object, verb' sequence. For example, to say 'I like hiking' in Japanese, the sentence is structured, 'I hiking like' (*watashi wa haikingu ga suki desu* 私はハイキングが好きです).

There are three writing systems in Japan:

Kanji – these are Chinese characters (ideograms), introduced to Japan in the fifth century. An understanding of at least 2000 to 3000 is needed to read a Japanese newspaper. Unlike Chinese, Japanese sentences cannot be written using *kanji* alone, but use a combination of the three writing systems. Examples of *kanji* are: 女 (*onna*, woman), 男 (*otoko*, man), 川 (*kawa*, river), 山 (*yama*, mountain), 峠 (*toge*, mountain pass – combining the three *kanji* for mountain, up and down), 木 (*ki*, tree), 森 (*mori*, forest).

Hiragana and **katakana** – two syllabaries (a collection of characters representing syllables) consisting of 46 letters, established in the ninth century with Koba Daishi often attributed as the creator. Examples of *hiragana* include: はい (*hai*, yes), いいえ (*iie*, no), すみません (*sumimasen*, excuse me). *Katakana* has a number of functions but is mainly used for foreign and 'loan words'; for example, ハイキング (*haikingu*, hiking), バス (*basu*, bus), ビール (*beeru*, beer), コーヒー (*kou-hii*, coffee), パン (*pan*, bread – from the Portuguese *pão*). Understanding *katakana* will help with reading menus.

If you would like to learn some spoken or written Japanese before your trip, the following links provide free online lessons:
• www.nhk.or.jp/lesson/english
• www.bbc.co.uk/languages

Common Japanese words listed in this guide and their meanings can be found in the glossary in Appendix B.

CULTURAL ETIQUETTE

Bowing

In Japan, rather than hugging or shaking hands it's customary to bow when you meet someone, as well as when you want to say things like goodbye, thank you and sorry. To bow, bend from your hips with your arms by your side. The lower the bow, the more respect you're paying or being paid.

Shoes

Shoes are taken off and left at the entrance (and slippers provided) for most accommodation, shrines, temples, houses and even many restaurants. Never wear shoes or slippers on the *tatami* mats in your bedroom (and don't roll suitcases on the mats); there will be a space at the entrance of the room to leave your slippers. 'Inside' slippers are swapped for 'toilet' slippers for use in the bathroom. Only socks should be worn (or go barefoot) while walking on the *tatami* mats.

Buddhist priests crossing a bridge over the Hasu-ike (lotus pond) in Koyasan during a spring festival

Japanese accommodation

If staying in accommodation where you need to set out your own futon, don't sleep with your head facing north (this is associated with funerals).

Yukata are a type of dressing gown and are provided in most Japanese accommodation. You can wear these to dinner, around the establishment and to bed. The most important thing to remember when wearing the *yukata* is to fold the left side over the right then tie the belt (the opposite is a symbol of death).

Dining

- Never place your chopsticks upright in a bowl of rice; use the chopstick rests provided. Don't point with chopsticks, don't pass food with them and don't pass food from one set of chopsticks to

another. (These rituals are related to Buddhist funeral ceremonies.)

- It's considered rude to pour sauce onto your rice and to leave any rice remaining.
- Bring bowls of food to your mouth.
- Slurping is acceptable when eating noodles; it's a sign of appreciation and helps to cool them down.
- Avoid pouring your own drink; pour for the person sitting beside you and they'll pour yours.

Tipping

Tipping is not commonly practised in Japan and you may find the waiter/waitress chasing you down the street to hand it back. In many restaurants a cover charge is added automatically to the bill.

Toilets

There are traditional 'squat'-style toilets or hi-tech 'Western seat' style with remote controls. In public toilets (which are free of charge) you will often find both; in most homes and accommodation you'll find Western style, but there may be some occasions when the only option is the squat style. With the squat style, face the flushing handle. With the remote-control type, various buttons will activate the bidet (front or back), adjust the temperature and flow of the bidet water, make flushing sounds, and sometimes flush the toilet. Try the buttons if you dare!

Bathing

Onsen 温泉 (hot springs) and *sento* 銭湯 (public bathhouses) are a communal and social bathing experience, and unless using a private bath for couples, most have separate sections for men and women. Bathing costumes are not permitted except for the river baths in Kawayu Onsen. (Note that some bathhouses don't allow entry to people with tattoos. There is usually a sign at the entrance; if you have tattoos and they are discreet or you're able to cover them with a bandage, then this should be fine.) Hot spring water can change the colour of jewellery, so you may wish to remove it.

1   Enter through the appropriate *noren* (curtain, women: 女湯/men: 男湯).

2   Once in the dressing room, take off your clothes and put them in a locker or basket, then cover yourself with the small 'modesty' towel (often provided for free at your accommodation or *onsen*).

3   Move into the bath area, but before getting into the bath you must wash yourself (stools are provided to sit on).

4   Soak in the bath, making sure not to let your towel or hair into the water. (The temperature is often around 40°C, so take your time getting in.)

5   Use your modesty towel to wipe yourself down before entering the dressing room.

Other

•   It's considered rude to blow your nose in public; instead walk away from people or go to the bathroom.

•   If bringing presents from home, make sure they are gift-wrapped.

•   Note that Japanese names are written surname before first name.

How to worship at a shrine or temple

Enter the shrine grounds through the *torii* gate (bow once at the gate before entering and once when leaving), or the temple grounds through the *san-mon* gate. If visiting a shrine, walk along the sides of the approach path, keeping the middle area free for the *kami* (gods).

Jison-in Temple, Kudoyama (Choishimichi)

First, for both a shrine and temple visit, purify yourself at the *temizuya* (water purification basin):

1 Pick up the ladle in your right hand and pour water over the left hand.

2 Swap the ladle into your left hand and pour water over the right hand.

3 Put the ladle back into the right hand and pour some water into your left hand to rinse your mouth out (spit the water outside of the basin).

4 With the ladle still in the right hand, scoop up some water and angle the ladle so the water runs down the handle to clean it, then place the ladle back on the basin.

Shrines

1 Throw a coin into the offering box (the ¥5 coin is the most auspicious)

2 Ring the bell/gong, if there is one (to awaken the *kami*)

3 Bow twice

4 Clap twice

5 Pray

6 Bow once

Temples

(The method for worshipping at temples in Japan varies widely)

1 Light a candle or incense

2 Throw a coin into the offering box

3 Ring the bell/gong, if there is one

4 Pray

LEAVE NO TRACE

It will be hard not to notice how clean the streets and trails are in Japan, so please help to keep them this way by carrying out all of your rubbish, including banana skins and fruit peel. Zip-lock bags are handy for disposing of tissues/rubbish as you walk. When you do see a bin, they are usually divided into plastics/paper/cans and burnable for recycling. Please leave only footprints!

HIKING IN JAPAN

Hiking in Japan can be challenging (with the obvious language barrier) but is also a very rewarding and fulfilling experience. Where else can you bathe in a UNESCO World Heritage *onsen* at the end of a long day's hike? The main point to keep in mind on these Kumano Kodo trails is that the paths are often covered in tree roots with sections of slippery moss-covered flagstone and strenuous hills, meaning distances like 16.4km (Nakahechi Stage 1 from Takijiri-oji to Tsugizakura-oji) can take around 8–9 hours. Even if you're used to walking in excess of 4km per hour, you may be reduced to 2km per hour here, so plan accordingly and set out early.

The Kohechi has fewer obstacles underfoot compared to the Nakahechi, so it's easier to get a quicker pace going, but you also have to climb a 1000m+ mountain each day.

Snakes are common (see 'Wildlife' for more information) so keep alert. Consider wearing long trousers or even gaiters rather than shorts.

USEFUL TIPS

- If buying new shoes or boots, break them in at home and make sure they have good ankle support.
- Make sure your pack fits comfortably.
- Invest in trekking poles, which will help your knees on the steep descents.
- It's never too early to start getting fit! The fitter you are, the more enjoyable your experience will be.
- Consider learning some Japanese phrases and basic *kanji* – see the Language section in this guide as well as the glossary in Appendix B.
- If you've had no time to train before leaving for Japan, remember to take it easy and have a backup plan in case you need to skip a section.

WHAT TO TAKE

Pack light, bearing in mind that in the accommodation you'll likely be provided with toiletries (shampoo and soap) as well as a *yukata* (dressing gown) and access to a washing machine. Whatever you do, don't plan on buying shoes in Japan if you are a woman and wear anything larger than size 25cm (UK6.5/US9) or a man and wear anything over size 27cm (UK8.5/US9.5), as 'large sizes' are virtually impossible to find outside of the major cities.

The following is a general guide based on travelling between spring and autumn.

- **Essential items:** passport, travel insurance, credit cards and cash
- **Footwear:** sturdy boots or shoes with good ankle support as there are many kilometres of loose stones, moss-covered slippery rocks and tree roots. A second pair of shoes is unnecessary as shoes aren't permitted inside most accommodation (slippers are provided), unless you want to walk around in the evening in a pair of lightweight sandals or flip-flops.
- **Clothes:** three sets of socks and underwear is a handy rule: wear one, wash one, have a spare. One long-sleeved quick-drying

Kumano Kodo stamp box

shirt is all you need for walking and an evening top to change into while you wash the walking shirt. Trousers are recommended year-round, given the mosquitoes and snakes. A fleece is useful for cooler days, early mornings and evenings. A beanie and gloves will come in handy at the higher altitudes or in early spring/late autumn. *Yukatas* are often provided to sleep in but you might

55

want to take base layers or light-weight pyjamas to wear under-neath. Stay away from cotton for your hiking clothes; lightweight and quick-drying synthetics or merino are better.

- **Rainwear:** the rainy season is mid June to mid July and typhoon sea-son is from May to October, but expect rain at any time of the year and take a good breathable rain jacket/trouser combination or poncho. Don't forget a backpack cover and you may wish to also have a drybag liner inside your pack.
- **Backpack:** a good-fitting, com-fortable 33–40L pack and a light-weight daypack or cloth bag for walking around towns
- **Trekking poles:** strongly rec-ommended for the many steep descents, ascents and rocky terrain
- **Water:** whether you like to use a bladder or a reusable plastic or metal bottle, ensure you have something to carry 1–2L of water
- **Headlamp and spare batteries:** useful as a safety precaution if you get caught in the mountains after dark
- **Towel:** most accommodations provide small 'modesty' towels the size of a tea towel; if you'd prefer something bigger, take a lightweight, quick-drying com-pact towel
- **Electronics:** take a travel adaptor if travelling from abroad (Japanese plugs are type A, two-flat-pin plugs, the same as in the US)
- **First-aid kit:** a compact kit includ-ing plasters, antiseptic cream, scissors and tweezers
- **Toiletries:** shampoo and soap are often provided. Take tissues, sun-screen, lip-balm, sanitary prod-ucts and antibacterial hand-gel.
- **Other gear:** hat, sunglasses, buff/scarf, zip-lock bags (for rubbish), spork (if you can't use chop-sticks), ear plugs, eye mask, nee-dle and thread (for blisters or sew-ing), mosquito repellent, bathing costume (not permitted in *onsen* or public baths), Japanese phrase-book or translation app on your phone.

LUGGAGE TRANSFERS

Through Kumano Travel

If you use the local Tanabe Kumano Travel Agency (www.kumano-travel.com/en) to book your accommoda-tion in advance, you can also add the luggage shuttle service onto your booking. Daily prices start from around ¥1500, depending on the ser-vice provider and distance. If you've booked your accommodation sepa-rately but would still like to use a lug-gage shuttle service, you can book this in person at Kumano Travel in Tanabe, located on the street directly in front of Kii-Tanabe station. Open daily 9am–6pm, tel 0739-22-2180, www.tb-kumano.jp/en

Through a delivery company

Delivery companies are called *tak-kyubin* 宅急便. Yamato transport is the most popular delivery company in Japan (yellow logo with a black cat) and you can use this service to forward luggage from many places including airports, convenience stores and accommodation. Most lodgings have the forms you need to fill in and prices start from around ¥1000 depending on the size. In rural areas, the service may take a minimum of two days to arrive, so plan ahead if you decide to use this service. Information (in English) is available at www.global-yamato.com

WAYMARKING

Nakahechi route

The Nakahechi is well waymarked with wooden posts at 500m intervals and 'Not Kumano Kodo' signs at many junctions. Each post is numbered and shows the emergency numbers for police (110) and fire/medical emergency (119). Takijiri-oji is the official starting point of the Nakahechi (marker zero) and the numbers count up to 75 to reach Hongu. From Hongu (Ukegawa) to Kumano Nachi Taisha along the Kogumotori-goe and Ogumotori-goe sections of the Nakahechi, wooden posts count down from 54 to one.

Kumano Kodo waymark

Kohechi route

At the time of writing (spring 2018), the trail was mostly waymarked with bilingual wooden and sometimes stone directional signs with distances. The section between Totsukawa Onsen and Hongu also follows numbered Kannon statues. (Kannon is the Bodhisattva of mercy and compassion and it is believed Kannon has 33 manifestations, with each represented by a statue.)

Iseji route

The mountain passes encountered in this guide have numbered bilingual wooden posts at 100m intervals with emergency contact details. These are only on the mountain passes; efforts are being made to waymark the whole route but at the time of writing there were practically no signs from town to town.

MAPS AND GPS

In addition to the maps in this guide, recommended trail maps in English and at a larger scale can be downloaded free of charge from the following sites:

- **Nakahechi and Kohechi:** www. tb-kumano.jp/en (select 'Kumano Kodo', then 'Kumano Kodo Maps')
- **Koyasan's Choishimichi:** http:// eng.shukubo.net (under the 'Information Download' tab)
- **Iseji:** www.kodo.pref.mie.lg.jp/en (there is an online navigational GPS produced by Mie Prefecture accessible on mobile phones. There are also maps for download; the Japanese-only sketch book is the best map – and the only one that includes the whole route – but an understanding of written and spoken Japanese is essential)

Stone and wooden waymarks lead the way down from Obako-toge Pass (Kohechi, Stage 2)

There is a Japanese series of maps produced by Shobunsha; no. 51 in the 'mountain and plateau maps', called 'Yama to Kogen chizu 山と高原地図', is a 1:80,000 map of Koyasan and Kumano Kodo '高野山・熊野古道' that includes Koyasan trails, the Nakahechi, Kohechi, and other trails in the region. This map is available in bookstores throughout Japan, at www.amazon.co.jp, and also as a mobile phone app. The app is only available in Japanese and is called 山と高原地図ホーダイ – first download the app, then purchase the correct map (no. 51 for the Kumano Kodo and Koyasan). Once downloaded, the map can be used offline.

When hiking in Japan it is always wise to have the destination written down in Japanese so you can compare this to the signs you're passing or show a local, if necessary. Please make sure to arrive at your accommodation at the agreed time or before dark so as not to worry your hosts.

GPS

A GPS is not required for the Nakahechi but may provide peace of mind for the Kohechi. GPX tracks are available online if you would like to download them to a smartphone or tablet: www.cicerone.co.uk/972/GPX

STAYING HEALTHY AND SAFE

The most common types of hiking-associated health issues are dehydration, blisters, sprained ankles, knee injuries and a sore back – most of which can be prevented. For more serious incidents, the emergency services can be contacted as follows:

- Fire (*kaji* 火事) and medical emergencies (*kyukyu* 救急) – tel 119
- Police (*keisatsu* 警察) – tel 110

If you need to call 119, English interpreter services are available in some areas, but if possible ask a local to call on your behalf as the operator will need to know the nature of the call (fire *kaji* or medical emergency *kyukyu*), your location and name.

Japan Helpline operates a 24-hour nationwide English-language assistance service for the international community and can also help in an emergency situation: tel 0570-00-0911.

Dehydration

If you're in the Kii Peninsula from April to October, it's likely to be very humid and you can find yourself dehydrated with minimal exercise. Make sure to 'camel up' (drink as much water as you can) in the morning before leaving your accommodation and carry 1–2L depending on the distance you're walking. Remember to take regular sips throughout the day. Sports drinks like Aquarius and Pocari Sweat are available from shops or vending machines, but also consider taking some rehydration sachets or electrolyte tablets with you.

Blisters

Lightweight merino socks will help your feet breathe in what is often a damp and humid environment. Avoid wearing cotton socks. If you feel a hotspot, act immediately and cover the area with a plaster. At the end of the day if you have any blisters with fluid, after washing, try the 'threading' method by threading a sterilised needle then pull the needle through the blister and leave the thread hanging out overnight. This allows the fluid to wick out. Remove the thread the next day.

Sprained ankles and knee injuries

There are plenty of obstacles along the trails, including loose stones, tree roots and slippery moss-covered flagstone paths which makes twisting an ankle a real possibility. Make sure you have shoes/boots with good ankle support and consider taking ankle/knee braces. Trekking poles spread the load and your knees will thank you for the extra support.

Back pain

Carrying a poor-fitting and overloaded backpack can result in pain and injury, so take care to choose a comfortable backpack and resist the urge to overpack. If this hike is part of a longer trip to Japan and you have

A new trail along the Kohechi (Stage 3)

a suitcase with you, make use of the luggage transfers.

Getting lost

Always carry a map, have the telephone number of your accommodation and know the Japanese *kanji* for your destination in case you need to ask a local for directions.

Natural disasters

Japan is a natural disaster-prone country (volcanic eruptions, earthquakes, tsunamis, typhoons, landslides, floods) but is also very disaster-prepared. Make sure you have adequate travel insurance in the event you need to call upon it. There is a free app (in English) for earthquake early warnings and tsunami warnings, available for both iOS and Android phones, called 'Safety Tips'. After any natural disaster, monitor news channels like NHK. For more information, see www.jnto. go.jp/safety-tips

Tropical cyclones (*typhoon* 台風)

With around 25 per year in Japan, typhoons can occur from May to October with the majority arriving in August and September. They bring strong winds, high tides and heavy rain which can result in landslides and flooding in coastal and mountainous areas. Trains and flights may be cancelled. Monitor local weather forecasts (www.jma.go.jp – English-language option), and if a typhoon is approaching, avoid coastal and mountainous areas and stay inside (away from windows) when it does hit. After a typhoon has passed, check with local authorities to see if it is safe to hike before entering the mountains.

Earthquakes (*jishin* 地震)

The islands of Japan are located in the Pacific Ring of Fire and on the junction of four tectonic plates, resulting in over 1000 noticeable earthquakes per year. If you are inside a building during an earthquake, follow these guidelines:

- Stay away from any windows, hide under something like a table/desk and protect your head until the tremor subsides.
- After the tremor ceases, open a window or door so you can evacuate if needed.
- Make sure there are no fire hazards (eg cooking appliances or lit cigarettes).
- In case an earthquake happens at night, make sure you have access to a torch/headlamp.

If you are outside during an earthquake, move away from any buildings/walls/electrical wires and anything that could fall down, and if you can't move to an open space, crouch down and protect your head. In the event of a major earthquake, follow the locals and head to the nearest evacuation area; this may be a park or school, depending on the location.

Tsunami 津波

After an earthquake there may be a risk of a tsunami. Look out for signs on electricity poles indicating your elevation above sea level, as well as signs directing you to areas/buildings that you should retreat to immediately in the event of a tsunami; otherwise move to higher ground immediately.

Sirens

Hongu, due to its location beside the Kumano-gawa River, has a set of warning sirens used to indicate that water will be released from the upstream dam. The sirens begin 30 minutes before the release. If unsure of any sirens or what action to take, please ask a local.

Wildlife

There are a few creatures to be aware of while hiking in this region.

Insects

*   **Japanese giant hornet** (*suzume-bachi* スズメバチ/雀蜂) *Vespa mandarinia japonica* – belonging to the Asian giant hornet family, they can grow to around 5cm and have a 6mm stinger. It's commonly thought they're attracted to black, so avoid dark clothing. Stings can be fatal: if stung, seek immediate medical attention.
*   **Giant centipede** (*mukade* ムカデ/百足) of the *Scolopendra subspinipes* family – a centipede with a black body and orange legs that can grow up to 20cm long. Especially active in the warmer months; check your shoes before putting them on. Bites are said to

be incredibly painful and reactions depend on the individual. If bitten, seek immediate medical attention.

*   **Ticks** (*madani* マダニ) *Ixodes scapularis* – tick-borne diseases are on the rise in Japan; try to prevent the risk of being bitten by covering up while walking (long sleeves and trousers) and wear light-coloured clothing so you can see any that may latch on.

Snakes

There are around 47 species in Japan but just two venomous snakes in this region.

*   **Japanese pit viper** (*mamushi* マムシ/蝮) *Gloydius blomhoffii* – the colour of the *mamushi* can vary from brown to grey but they have roundish dark blotches on their back, a diamond head and are typically 40–60cm long. Bites can be fatal depending on the individual; if bitten, seek immediate medical attention.
*   **Tiger keelback** (*yamakagashi* ヤマカガシ) *Rhabdophis tigrinis* – this snake is thought to be less aggressive and can often be identified by yellow colouring around the head and tiger-like colouring along its upper olive-dark-coloured body. If bitten, seek immediate medical attention.

Mammals

*   **Japanese black bear** (*tsuki no waguma* ツキノワグマ) *Ursus*

Dangerous wildlife: *Japanese giant hornet* (suzumebachi), *giant centipede* (mukade), *tiger keelback snake* (yamakagashi), *Japanese pit viper* (mamushi)

thibetanus japonicas – a member of the Asiatic black bear family, this bear is found in Honshu and Shikoku, grows to 120–140cm and can weigh up to 100kg (females) and 120kg (males). They are black with a white crescent-shaped patch of fur on their chest, thus their Japanese name, 'moon bear'. Carry a bear bell when walking any of Koyasan's trails, the Kohechi and in the mountains on the Iseji. If encountered, advice in Japan varies from stand

your ground to quietly and slowly retreat, but everyone agrees that you should carry a bear bell on the above-mentioned trails.

• **Wild boar** (*inoshishi* イノシシ/猪) *Sus scrofa leucomystax* – telltale signs of wild boar are upturned earth (they eat earthworms, insects, bamboo shoots and mushrooms) and electric fences around crops. Although usually skittish, they can weigh up to 70kg and if confronted or threatened, they can charge, using their tusks to inflict damage. Carry a bear bell so as not to catch any unawares.

Medicines and pharmacies

Medicine is called *kusuri* and is written as 薬 or くすり. Pharmacies in Japan are called *yakkoku* 薬局 and are found in most towns (Koyasan, Hongu, Tanabe, Shingu, Nachi-Katsuura...). Drug stores, *doraggu sutoa* ドラッグストア, are usually large stores with longer opening hours in towns/cities and sell a variety of products including supermarket goods as well as over-the-counter medicines. Convenience stores sell basic first-aid items and some over-the-counter medicines. Many Western brands of medicine are not available in Japan, but you can find Tylenol タイレノール (containing paracetamol), Bufferin バファリン (containing aspirin) and Ibuprofen イブプロフェン (pronounced *ibu-purofen*). For insect bites there is a gel called Kayumi-dome かゆみどめ (meaning 'stop itching') and medicine for diarrhoea is called Geri-dome 下痢止め (meaning 'stop diarrhoea'). Always check the ingredients on the label before consuming.

Note that Japan has strict zero-tolerance laws regarding bringing in drugs, including but not limited to some cold/flu/allergy/sinus medications, medicine containing pseudoephedrine and painkillers containing codeine. Check with the Japanese embassy in your country in advance if you're unsure of what you can take in with you. The following website has a list of embassies: www.mofa.go.jp (go to 'About Us', then 'Embassies & Consulates').

Vaccinations

No specific vaccinations are required for a trip to Japan, but make sure you're up to date with the usual vaccinations offered in your country. For more information see https://travelhealthpro.org.uk

USING THIS GUIDE

Each stage begins with an information box giving the start/finish points, distance, total ascent/descent, difficulty rating (easy, moderate or hard – based on a combination of distance, ascent and walking time), duration, access, waymarks and special notes. Distances for bus stops are cumulative; for example, 'Nonaka Ipposugi bus stop (16.4km +0.9km)' indicates that the bus stop is a 900m detour off the trail and that you leave the trail 16.4km from the start of the stage.

Following the information box is an introduction with an overview of the stage, and then detailed route directions. Stage maps at a scale of 1:50,000 are provided, as well as elevation profiles and larger scale town maps (towns that have a separate map are shown in **bold** on the stage map). Points of interest along the way are noted, as are any facilities that you may pass. Accommodation prices when stated are based on starting prices for one person. (All prices

A hiker on the trail after leaving Takahara (Nakahechi, Stage 1)

are accurate at the time of writing in spring 2018.) Keywords in **bold** in the route description relate to features that you will also see on the town and route maps for that stage, so you can cross-reference where you are. Coloured text is used to highlight accommodation, cafés/restaurants or other facilities.

Note that detours are sometimes put in place to divert the trails around landslides. Always follow new signs where applicable. Every effort has been made to provide up-to-date, accurate and clear directions, and further updates will be posted online at www.cicerone.co.uk/972/updates

Spellings and abbreviations

The following abbreviations have been used:

- LHS – left-hand side
- RHS – right-hand side
- VM – vending machine
- D&B – dinner and breakfast

Although not grammatically correct, names of bridges/rivers/shrines and mountain passes have been written as they are mostly seen on English signs, with the Japanese word followed by the English. For example:

- Kowase-bashi bridge – *bashi* is Japanese for bridge, so technically this says 'Kowase bridge bridge'. This also applies to the following examples:
- Kumano-gawa River – *gawa* means river
- Tokei-jinja Shrine – *jinja* means shrine
- Sakura-toge pass – *toge* means mountain pass
- Waroda-ishi rock – *ishi* means rock (or stone)

Nakahechi Stage 2 - a hiker and Kumano Kodo sign

- Seiganto-ji Temple – *ji* means temple (*do* and *in* are also suffixes for temple)

English spellings of Japanese words are also often inconsistent, with the use of '*h*', '*oo*' or '*ō*' for a long vowel, for example; to alleviate any confusion when comparing this guide with local maps and signs, local spellings have been used.

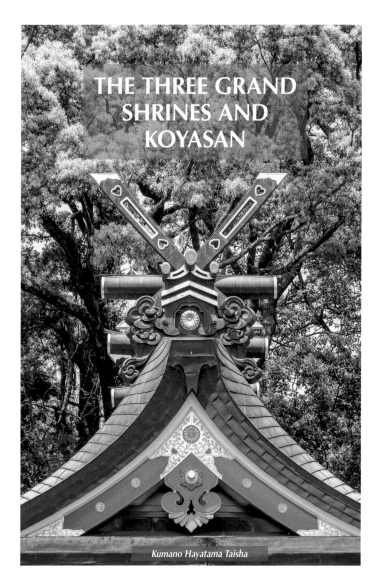

THE THREE GRAND SHRINES AND KOYASAN

Kumano Hayatama Taisha

THE THREE GRAND SHRINES
AND KOYASAN

With their origins in nature worship, the three grand shrines, known as the Kumano Sanzan, also symbolise the past (Kumano Hayatama Taisha), present (Kumano Nachi Taisha), and future (Kumano Hongu Taisha). By worshipping at all three, one is thought to find salvation, peace and good luck for each realm.

KUMANO HONGU TAISHA
熊野本宮大社

The current location of Kumano Hongu Taisha, on a hillside reached by a flight of stone steps, dates from 1891 after the original complex at Oyunohara was destroyed in a flood. The unassuming wooden buildings with cypress-bark thatched roofs are surrounded by forest and enshrine four of the 12 Kumano deities. The main deity is Ketsumiko-no-Okami, a Shinto manifestation of the Buddha of Infinite Light, Amida Nyorai. The shrine's annual spring festival is well worth a visit – particularly the last day on 15 April when there's a colourful and lively procession of people in traditional costume carrying *mikoshi* portable shrines to Oyunohara.

Highlights of the shrine include the painting of the original complex at Oyunohara opposite the *temizuya*

Looking through the shinmon gate to Kumano Hongu Taisha's main sanctuary (water purification basin) almost at the top of the stairs. In the grounds, notice the unique black post box crowned with the Yatagarasu (three-legged crow) with a Tarayou holly tree (*Ilex latifolia*) behind it. These trees are often found in shrines and temples and it's thought in days gone by, sutras were written on the leaves. Indeed, the Japanese name for postcard is *hagaki* (leaf write). Finally, at the entrance to the *honden* (main sanctuary) is the large *shinmon* (gate) draped with a thick *shimenawa* (sacred Shinto rope) and curtain with the imperial family's chrysanthemum crest as well as featuring the current zodiac animal. A sign near the gate describes the order in which to worship at each of the four shrines.

Amulets for luck and protection can be bought at the amulet office, which also sells the special Kumano Goohoin paper talisman. The *homotsuden* (treasure hall) is open daily 10am–4pm with a small entry fee.

The original Kumano Kodo route is parallel to the flight of flag-lined stone steps. If heading downhill, the path can be accessed on the RHS, just up from the water purification basin.

HONGU 本宮, 69M, POP 546

A small town by the Kumano-gawa River and surrounded by mountains, the settlement stretches along Route 168 with Kumano Hongu Taisha at the northern end and the Dainichi-goe trailhead for Yunomine Onsen to the south. In between are a handful of accommodation options, the excellent Kumano Hongu Heritage Center, a post office/ATM, cafés and restaurants (mostly only open for lunch), pharmacies and a convenience store. From time to time in rural areas you may hear music played over the speaker system to denote certain times of the day, for example, Hongu has a short jingle at 12pm (lunch time) and 5pm (the end of the working day). Due to its location beside the Kumano-gawa River, Hongu also has a set of warning sirens used to indicate that water will be released from the upstream dam. The sirens begin 30 minutes before the release. If unsure of any sirens or what action to take, please ask a local.

Access: serviced by buses from Tanabe, Shingu, Totsukawa Onsen and more, the main bus stop is Hongu-taisha-mae 本宮大社前 バス停 in front of Kumano Hongu Taisha. For the nearby spa resorts of Yunomine, Wataze and Kawayu, as well as Tanabe, Shingu and Koyasan, buses depart from outside the Kumano Hongu Heritage Center. For Hosshinmon-oji (Nakahechi route), Yakio (Kohechi route) or Totsukawa Onsen, buses depart on the other side of the road beside the main entrance to Kumano Hongu Taisha.

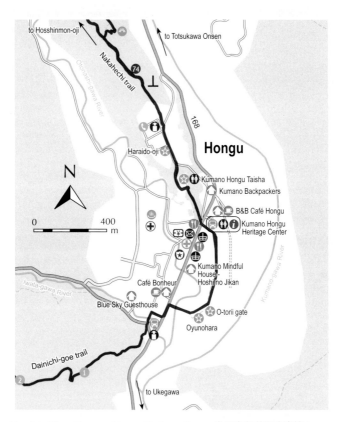

Tourist office: Kumano Hongu Heritage Center 世界遺産 熊野本宮館 is two buildings with a tourism office, Kumano Kodo exhibitions, wi-fi, WC, electric bicycle rental and English-speaking staff. Open daily 8.30am–5pm, tel 0735-42-0751, www.city.tanabe.lg.jp/hongukan/en

Visit: in addition to **Kumano Hongu Taisha** and the **Kumano Hongu Heritage Center** (described above), no visit to Hongu could be complete without visiting **Oyunohara** 大斎原 – the original shrine complex (first referenced in AD859). Located on a sandbank between two rivers, the site is now surrounded by trees

Traditional kawabune boats

and rice paddies, protected from what was once the raging Kumano-gawa River to the east by a flood bank. Until the Edo period, reaching the shrine required one last act of purification, wading through the (smaller) Otonashi-gawa River. These days there is a bridge and in fact most people enter through Japan's largest *torii* gate (a *torii* is a gate marking the boundary of the sacred and secular worlds), called O-torii. Eight of the 12 Kumano deities are still enshrined here within two stone monuments (the other four were moved to the new complex).

Kumano-gawa River pilgrimage: the Kumano-gawa River runs for 183km from Mt Omine to the Pacific Ocean at Shingu. The section between Hongu and Shingu is included in the World Heritage listing; retired emperors and nobles would traditionally travel this section on a boat called a *kawabune*. While the river holds a fraction of the water it once did due to damming, you can still travel downstream on a traditional boat to Kumano Hayatama Taisha. Guided boat tours run twice daily (Mar–Nov) at 10am and 2.30pm, taking 90min and costing around ¥3900pp. The departure point is the Kawabune River Boat Tour Center 熊野川 川舟センター (bus stop: Michi-no-eki Kumano-gawa 道の駅 熊野川 バス停, 50min from Hongu or 30min from Shingu). Advance bookings are recommended through Kumano Travel www.kumano-travel.com/en (search 'Tours & Activities'; 'River').

Where to eat: many of the restaurants in Hongu are only open for lunch and the Y-shop convenience store closes at 7pm. Café Bonheur カフェ ボヌール is a vegan café/restaurant on the main road run by a lovely couple who prepare flavoursome food using locally sourced produce (try the curry!). The café is open for dinner by prior reservation only. B&B Café Hongu, opposite the entrance to Kumano Hongu Taisha, serves tasty meals including Japanese curry, pasta and cakes. There are a few popular noodle restaurants that serve tasty set meals, including Otonashi jaya おとなし茶屋 (on the corner before the post office) and Shimoji しもじ本宮店 (in front of the Konan hardware store). For snacks and ready-made meals there is a Y-shop convenience store (opposite the post office) and the Konan hardware store for bread, snacks, drinks and pot noodles.

Accommodation: Blue Sky Guesthouse 蒼空げすとはうす (tel 0735-42-0800, www.kumano-guesthouse.com/eng.html, four rooms, ¥¥ incl breakfast.

Located a few minutes' walk from the Dainichi-goe trailhead, this modern Japanese guesthouse is surrounded by forest). **B&B Cafe Hongu** (tel 0735-42-1130, **www.kumano-experience.com/WP2017/en**, four Western-style rooms above the café, ¥¥¥ incl D&B, opposite the main entrance to Kumano Hongu Taisha). **Kumano Backpackers** くまのバックパッカーズ (tel 0735-42-0220, **www. kumano-experience.com/WP2017/en**, bunk-bed dorms and one private room with a communal bathroom, kitchen and dining areas, ¥, located a stone's throw from Kumano Hongu Taisha). **Café Bonheur** カフェ ボヌール (tel 0735-42-1833, **www.bonheurcompany.com**, rent an entire house that has been lovingly restored, ¥¥¥ including dinner; or stay in one of their three guesthouse rooms, ¥¥ including dinner). **Kumano Mindful House – Hoshi no Jikan** 熊野マインドフルハウス 星の時間 (tel 090-8822-2050, **www.mindfulretreat.jp/kumanohouse**, ¥¥¥¥, a rental house for up to six people located on the main street (Route 168) opposite Oyunohara's O-torii gate).

KUMANO HAYATAMA TAISHA
熊野速玉大社

Located on the bank of the Kumano-gawa River in Shingu (a 15min walk from the station), this *shin-gu* (new shrine) was built in the 12th century to replace the original site of worship at the nearby Kamikura-jinja Shrine. Kumano Hayatama Taisha is striking with its vermilion-coloured buildings

Kumano Hayatama Taisha's shinmon gate

set against a forest backdrop. A stone monument next to the amulet office has the names of each imperial member and the number of times they visited, totalling 141. The main deity is Hayatama-no-Okami, a Shinto manifestation of the Buddha of medicine and healing, Yakushi Nyorai.

Within the grounds there's a large sacred podocarpus nagi tree (*nagi-no-ki*), a designated Natural Monument. Some say it's over 1000 years old, others say it was planted by Taira no Shigemori (1138–1179), but there's no doubting it's old! Pilgrims would traditionally take a leaf for their onward journey for good luck;

nowadays amulets made with the tree's nuts called *nagi-mamori* are sold here, in addition to the popular Kumano Goohoin paper talisman. Next to the sacred tree there's a copy of the Hayatama pilgrimage *mandala* (spiritual iconography, in this case a painting depicting the Kumano River pilgrimage, Kamikura-jinja Shrine (the fire-dragon cascading down the steps depicts the February fire festival) and Asuka-jinja Shrine), and the treasure house (modest entry fee) contains relics including sutra cases, pottery, mirrors, Buddhist images, scrolls and swords, but unfortunately no English translations.

SHINGU 新宮, 11M, POP 29,276

Facing the Pacific Ocean and located at the mouth of the Kumano-gawa River, Shingu is home to one of the Kumano grand shrines, Kumano Hayatama Taisha, from which the city takes its name. A castle town during the Edo period, Shingu is known today for its timber and paper industries.

Access: in addition to arriving by traditional boat (see 'Kumano-gawa River pilgrimage' in the Hongu section), it is possible to access Shingu via bus from neighbouring areas including Nachi-Katsuura, Hongu, Totsukawa Onsen and Kumano City; the bus station is located opposite Shingu station 新宮駅. Shingu is on the JR Kisei main line. Express trains run to Osaka (4hr 30min, via Kii-Katsuura, Kii-Tanabe, Wakayama) or Nagoya (3hr 30min, via Kumanoshi, Owase and more)

Tourist office: Shingu City Tourist Information Center 熊野新宮観光案内センター opposite Shingu station has English-speaking staff, maps, bus/train timetables and bicycle rental. Open daily 9am–5pm, tel 0735-22-2840, www.shinguu.jp/en

Visit: Kamikura-jinja Shrine 神倉神社 and **Gotobiki-iwa rock** ゴトビキ岩 – the original shrine, nestled underneath the towering Gotobiki-iwa rock halfway up Mt Gongen, at the top of 538 precipitous stone steps, is said to be where the Kumano gods first descended from heaven. Relics of a third-century bronze bell

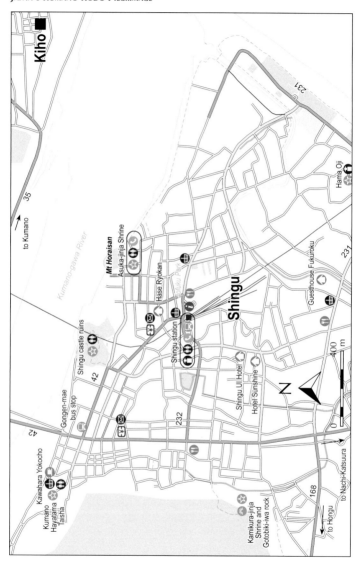

Kiho

to Kumano

35

Kumano-gawa River

to Kumano

42

Shingu castle ruins

Gongen-mae bus stop

42

Kawahara Yokocho

Kumano Hayatama Taisha

232

Mt Horaisan
Asuka-jinja Shrine

Hase Ryokan

Jofuku Park

Shingu station

Shingu

Shingu UI Hotel

Hotel Sunshine

N

Kamikura-jinja Shrine and Gotobiki-iwa rock

168

to Hongu

to Nachi-Katsuura

Guesthouse Fukuroku

231

Hama Oji

231

0   400   m

and 12th-century sutra mounds have been discovered around Gotobiki-iwa rock (meaning 'toad'), the main object of worship. You can get right up to it and feel its energy while simultaneously taking in the expansive view of Shingu and the Pacific Ocean. The stone steps, which were donated by Minamoto Yoritomo (1147–1199), are at their steepest and narrowest at the very beginning of the climb; it's incredible to think that there's an annual festival (Oto Matsuri, 6 February) when 2000 men run down the steps carrying fire torches! At the base of the mountain before crossing the short bridge, notice the stone marker (RHS, dated 1672) advising people to dismount their horses '下馬'. **Asuka-jinja Shrine** 阿須賀神社, located at the base of Mt Horai – relics from the Yayoi (300BC–AD250) and Kofun (AD250–552) periods have been discovered here and there is a museum adjacent. **Shingu castle ruins** 新宮城跡, built between 1601–1633 and used until the Meiji period – not much remains but it's a popular cherry blossom viewing area in spring. **Jofuku Park** 徐福公園, located near the station with a bright Chinese gate at the entrance – the park commemorates a legendary man called Jofuku who was sent from China around 2200 years ago to find the 'elixir of life'. Jofuku found a special herb instead (*tendai uyaku*), settled in Shingu, was buried here and the gravestone was donated by the Kishu Lord Tokugawa Yorinobu (1602–1671).

Where to eat: Jofuku zushi 徐福寿司 opposite Shingu station serves local sushi dishes including *sanma-zushi* and *mehari-zushi*, open daily except Thursdays 10am–5pm. Chukasoba Hayami 中華そば 速水, located near Guesthouse Fukuroku, serves Wakayama Ramen, open daily except Thursday afternoons, 11.30am–2pm & 5.30–9.30pm. Kawahara Yokocho 川原家横丁 is a collection of traditional wooden shops next to Kumano Hayatama Taisha selling local products and snacks. Tanukiya たぬき屋 is a noodle restaurant on Route 42 a few minutes' walk from Kamikura-jinja Shrine, open 11am–8pm. There is also a Lawson convenience store opposite the station, and an Okuwa supermarket オークワ 500m from the station.

Accommodation: options are not as plentiful in Shingu as the nearby *onsen* resort of Nachi-Katsuura (details in Nachi-Katsuura section), but if the following are full, ask at the tourist office for more options. Guesthouse Fukuroku ふくろく (tel 090-5093-6445, **www.booking.com**, two rooms, ¥, the guesthouse is a 10min walk from Shingu station but a pickup can be arranged by the owner. There is a Lawson convenience store and a handful of restaurants in the immediate vicinity). Shingu UI Hotel 新宮ユーアイホテル (tel 0735-22-6611, **www.ui-hotel.co.jp**, 84 (Western- and Japanese-style) rooms, ¥¥, a nice hotel with onsite restaurant, 8min walk from the station). Hotel Sunshine 新宮サンシャインホテル (tel 0735-23-2580, **www.sunshinenet.co.jp/hotel/en**, 43 Western-style rooms, ¥¥, a business hotel 10min walk from the station). Hase Ryokan 長谷旅館 (tel 0735-22-2185, **www.booking.com**, 14 Western- and Japanese-style rooms, ¥¥, an older-style *ryokan* with simple rooms in a convenient location a few minutes from the station).

KUMANO NACHI TAISHA
熊野那智大社

Kumano Nachi Taisha, located half-way up Nachisan (Mt Nachi), traces its origin to the worship of Nachi Falls. The shrine buildings are said to have been moved to their current location from beside the falls in the fourth century, and most recently rebuilt in 1853. The legendary Emperor Jimmu (who ascended the throne around 660BC) is believed to have discovered the falls while being guided by the three-legged Yatagarasu crow to Yamato (present-day Nara), and

they have been worshipped ever since. Kumano Nachi Taisha's main deity is Fusumi-no-Okami, a Shinto manifestation of the thousand-armed Bodhisattva of mercy and compassion, Senju Kannon.

The excellent treasure house (small entry fee, open daily 8.30am–4pm) contains a Nachi pilgrimage painted *mandala* (iconography, the like of which *bikuni* travelling nuns used to spread the faith of the Kumano region around Japan), sutra cases and relics from the 12th century onwards that were excavated

Torii gate and staircase leading to Kumano Nachi Taisha

from sutra mounds at the base of the falls, and is the only treasury house of the three grand shrines to have English translations. There are a number of sacred trees in the grounds including a *shidare-zakura* (weeping cherry tree) believed to be planted by former emperor Go-Shirakawa (1127–1192) and a large camphor tree planted by Taira no Shigemori (1138–1179); you can even walk through its hollow trunk! Within the inner sanctuary there is a sacred *karasu-ishi* stone which the Yatagarasu crow is believed to have transformed into.

NACHISAN 那智山, 368M, POP 112

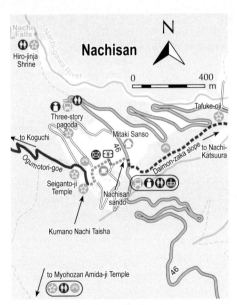

This mountainside religious complex is a perfect example of Shinto-Buddhist syncretism; Seiganto-ji Temple stands next to the Shinto Kumano Nachi Taisha, and the best views of Nachi Falls (the origin of the shrine's worship) are from the three-storey pagoda (Buddhist architecture). The religious buildings were destroyed in the 16th century by the warlord Oda Nobunaga, then rebuilt in 1590 by his successor, Toyotomi Hideyoshi. There is a post office/ATM, accommodation, cafés, and souvenir shops lining the Nachisan *sando* (shrine steps) selling products made from the local charcoal called Kishu-Binchotan, produced from the indigenous *ubame* oak (*Quercus phillyraeoides*).

Access: the area is serviced by buses from Kii-Katsuura (25min) and Nachi (17min) stations, and there are three main bus stops in the vicinity: Daimonzaka 大門坂 バス停 – at the base of Daimonzaka slope, get off here if you want to walk up Daimonzaka to Kumano Nachi Taisha, 1.3km; Nachi-no-Taki mae 那智の滝前 バス停 – the closest to Nachi Falls, get off here and walk down the 200m stone path to the falls; and Nachisan 那智山 バス停 – the closest to Kumano Nachi Taisha (400m), at the bottom of the Nachisan *sando* (shrine steps).

Visit: Seiganto-ji Temple 那智山 青岸渡寺 – in the fourth century (two centuries before the arrival of Buddhism in Japan), a Buddhist priest from India called Ragyo Shonin arrived on the peninsula and followed the Nachi-gawa River to the emanating light of the falls. While standing under the falls one day a small statue of Kannon (the Bodhisattva of mercy and compassion) appeared, so he built a hermitage to enshrine the Kannon. This is believed to be the origin of Seiganto-ji Temple, which is number one on the 33 Kannon pilgrimage. The current building is the 16th-century reconstruction. There's a Hokyo-in stupa on the RHS of the temple (with the date 1322 carved into it by a Buddhist nun), and a morning ceremony is held daily at 5am. **Nachi Falls** (Nachi-no Otaki) 那智の滝 – the largest waterfall in Japan (133m), it is revered as the deity 'Hiro Gongen' and has long been a site for Shugendo mountain ascetic practices. The sacred *shimenawa* rope hung over the top of the falls is replaced in a festival twice a year (9 July & 27 December). At the base of the falls there is a shrine called **Hiro-jinja** 飛瀧神社, a viewing platform (open 7am–4.30pm, small entry fee), and a place to taste the water, said to bring longevity (you can purchase a ceramic saucer for ¥100). The stone path leading to the falls between cedar trees is called Otakimichi and is thought to have been laid in the Kamakura period under the orders of Minamoto Yoritomo (1147–1199). Sutra mounds were discovered around the base in 1918 and relics can be seen in the treasure hall. The forest to the east is primeval. **Three-storey pagoda** 三重の塔 – halfway between Kumano Nachi Taisha and the falls is the three-storey vermillion-coloured pagoda first built at the end of the Heian period (794–1185) and rebuilt in 1972. Pagodas are a Buddhist style of architecture evolved from Indian stupas that were constructed to house sacred relics. There are unrivalled views of the falls from the top, open 8.30am–4pm, small entry fee. **Daimonzaka** 大門坂 – a 600m flagstone slope lined with ancient cedar trees and the last *oji* (Tafuke-oji). The name means 'large gate slope', as there was once a gate at the top marking the boundary between the sacred and secular worlds. Pilgrims walking up this slope from the coast were awarded their first view of Nachi Falls 200m from the top – there are a couple of benches and a Japanese sign marking this site as an old checkpoint '十一文関跡'. Daimonzaka-chaya

teahouse 大門坂茶屋 at the base of the Daimonzaka stairs rents traditional Heian costumes (¥2000+pp) and provides two stamps, one for Tafuke-oji and the other a beautiful large purple stamp of Daimonzaka. If approaching from Kumano Nachi Taisha (walking downhill), the Daimonzaka entrance is near Nachisan bus stop. 'Daimonzaka' bus stop is at the base of the slope.

Three-storey pagoda and Nachi Falls

Where to eat: there are numerous cafés surrounding the complex which are open for lunch, but none in more of an historic setting than Seiryotei teahouse 清涼亭 in the courtyard of Jippo-in, the former accommodation for abdicated emperors during their pilgrimages. The garden also has a great cleyera tree, 10m high, 1.8m wide and thought to be over 400 years old, as well as lovely views. Located on the Nachisan *sando* (shrine steps to Kumano Nachi Taisha).

Accommodation: Mitaki Sanso 美滝山荘 (www.mitaki-sanso.com (Japanese site), 13 rooms, ¥¥¥ incl D&B. This is the only accommodation on the mountain and is in a privileged location; some rooms have views of the falls and the meals are excellent).

NACHI-KATSUURA 那智勝浦, 4M, POP 15,490

A coastal town known for its hot springs and Japan's largest fresh catch of tuna, Nachi-Katsuura is brimming with accommodation and sushi restaurants.

The harbour and fish market in Nachi-Katsuura

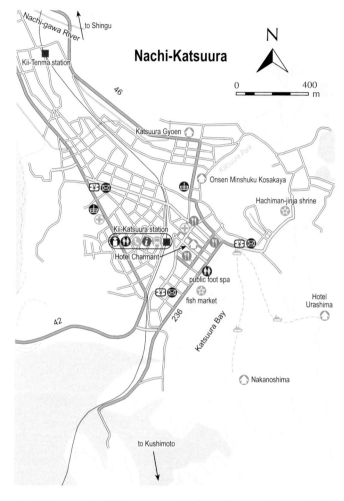

Access: buses service Kii-Katsuura from Nachi, Nachisan and Shingu; the bus station is opposite Kii-Katsuura station 紀伊勝浦駅. Kii-Katsuura is on the JR Kisei main line. Express trains run to Osaka (4hr, via Kii-Tanabe, Wakayama, among others) or Nagoya (4hr, via Shingu, Kumanoshi and others).

Tourist office: Nachi-Katsuura Tourist Information Center 那智勝浦町観光協会 (on the ground floor of Kii-Katsuura station) has English-speaking staff, maps, bus/train timetables and bicycle rental. Open daily 8.30am–6pm, tel 0735-52-5311, **www.nachikan.jp/en**. There is a local area accommodation booking office next door.

Visit: Tuna Auctions, held Sun–Fri from 7am, there's an observation deck on the second floor. **Sunday market nigiwai hiroba** にぎわい広場, held beside the fish market, 8–11am. The nearby island *onsen* resorts provide free ferry transport and day-use of the *onsen* is possible.

Where to eat: Meharizushi Nidaime めはり寿司 二代目 has good set menus with *mehari-zushi*, tuna and *kushi-katsu* fried skewers). Ichirin いちりん, a popular Japanese *izakaya* (pub) opposite Hotel Charmant. Ogawa おがわ, a sushi restaurant close to the harbour.

Accommodation: Hotel Charmant ホテルシャルモント (tel 0735-52-0203, 15 Western-style rooms, ¥¥ room only, located a stone's throw from the station, the owners couldn't be more helpful in this hotel that has everything you could ever need). Onsen Minshuku Kosakaya 温泉民宿小阪屋 (tel 0735-52-0335, **www.kosakaya.jp** (Japanese site), 16 rooms, ¥¥¥ incl D&B, convenient modern accommodation opposite the Family Mart). Katsuura Gyoen かつうら御苑 (tel 0735-52-0333, **www.katuuragyoen.co.jp** (English-language option), 89 (Western- and Japanese-style) rooms, ¥¥¥¥¥ incl D&B, a luxury *onsen* hotel beside the sea). The following two *onsen* hotels are located on private islands a few minutes' ferry ride from Katsuura Port: Hotel Urashima ホテル浦島 (tel 0735-52-1011, **www.hotelurashima.co.jp/en**, an enormous hotel with Western- and Japanese-style rooms spread over four buildings, ¥¥¥¥ incl D&B). Nakanoshima 中の島 (tel 0735-52-1111, **www.hotel-nakanoshima.jp/en**, 31 (Western- and Japanese-style) rooms, ¥¥¥¥¥ incl D&B, large hotel with tunnel access between buildings).

KOYASAN 高野山

Koyasan, in an alpine basin surrounded by eight peaks (believed to resemble a lotus flower) is home to the headquarters of the Shingon school of Esoteric Buddhism, established by Kobo Daishi in AD816. The main sights are at opposite ends of town; to the east is Kobo Daishi's mausoleum in the inner sanctuary/cemetery called

Okunoin, and in the west the Danjo Garan temple complex. There are 117 temples, 52 of which offer accommodation, and all the facilities you would expect for a popular tourist town.

Kobo Daishi 弘法大師

The history of Koyasan begins with a man named Kukai (774–835), posthumously called Kobo Daishi. Born on the island of Shikoku, Kobo Daishi became a Buddhist monk at the age of 20. In 804 he travelled to Xian and met with the Chinese master Huiguo, who passed on the teachings of Shingon Mikkyo Esoteric Buddhism (meaning 'true word'). Two years later he returned to Japan but before setting sail, legend has it, he threw a three-pronged *vajra* (Buddhist ritual implement) into the sky, praying for it to guide him to the sacred location

where he should establish his Shingon school.

While walking through the mountains one day in Japan, Kobo Daishi came across the Shinto god Kariba Myojin disguised as a hunter with two dogs (one black and one white). The hunter told him to follow his dogs and they would lead him to the place he had been searching for. Along the way, he met Niutsuhime, the Shinto guardian of the area, and she gave him permission to continue. In Koyasan he found the three-pronged *vajra* thrown from China resting in a three-needle pine tree (this *sanko-no-matsu* pine tree stands in the grounds of the Danjo Garan complex) and knew he had found what he was looking for. In 816 he was granted permission from the emperor to establish the Shingon School of Esoteric Buddhism

An illustration in the grounds of Niukanshofu-jinja Shrine showing the story of Kobo Daishi (Koyasan Choishimichi route)

Banryutei *rock garden at Kongobu-ji Temple*

on Koyasan and it was consecrated in 819. On 21 March 835, Kobo Daishi entered a state of eternal meditation and his mausoleum is located behind the Toro-do (Hall of Lanterns) in Okunoin.

Places to visit

At the western entrance (at the top of the Choishimichi path), **Daimon gate** 大門 is the main entrance to Koyasan, built in 1705 after the original burned down. It is a popular sunset viewpoint.

The **Danjo Garan sacred religious complex** 壇上伽藍 consists of 20 buildings and was the first area to be constructed by Kobo Daishi and his followers in the ninth century. Pick up a brochure from the tourist office for a more in-depth description of these sacred buildings. Highlights include:

- Konpon Daito 根本大塔 (the great pagoda) – a two-storey 48.5m tall vermillion pagoda built by Kobo Daishi and his successor Shinzen Daitoku from 816–887; the current building was reconstructed in 1937

- Daito Bell 大塔の鐘 – the copper bell was cast in 1547 and is rung five times a day

- Kondo 金堂 – Koyasan's main temple; construction began under Kobo Daishi in 819. The current building dates from 1932.

- Miei-do 御影堂 (great portrait hall) – this hall contains a ninth-century portrait of Kobo Daishi painted by Shinnon, one of his disciples. The current building dates from 1848.

- Miyashiro Shrine 御社 – dedicated to the guardian deities of the mountain Niutsuhime and Kariba Myojin, the current buildings were reconstructed in 1522

- Sanko-no-matsu 三鈷の松 ('three-needle pine tree') – encompassed by a vermillion fence and located between the Kondo and Miedo, this is believed to be the tree where Kobo Daishi's three-pronged *vajra* landed after he threw it from China in 806. The pine tree's needles are considered lucky, so you may see visitors scouring the ground for them.

There were originally two temples on the site of **Kongobu-ji Temple** 金剛峯寺 that merged to become one, the head temple of Koyasan's Shingon School. The rock garden in the grounds, *banryutei*, is the largest in Japan and depicts two dragons in a sea of clouds. Among the many beautiful rooms, the willow room is the most infamous; it was where Toyotomi Hidetsugu (1568–1595) committed ritual suicide under the orders of his step-uncle Toyotomi Hideyoshi (1537–1598). Open daily 8.30am–5pm, modest entry fee.

Okunoin 奥之院 (also written as 奥の院) is the inner sanctuary, home to the sacred site of Kobo Daishi's mausoleum, surrounded by three mountains. Enter the cemetery through the main entrance by crossing *ichinohashi* 一の橋 (the first bridge) then walk the 2km path called Okunoin-Sando 奥之院 参道, lined with lanterns, cedar trees of around 500-year-old, and over 200,000 gravestones. After crossing *nakano-hashi* 中の橋 (the middle bridge), there are steps on what is called the Kakuban-zaka slope 覚鑁坂; don't fall over here – it's believed that those who do will die within three years! Just before crossing the third and final bridge, *gobyo-bashi* 御廟橋 (mausoleum bridge), notice the Mizumuke Jizo 水向地蔵 (water Jizo statues, RHS – Jizo being a Bodhisattva that is considered the guardian of children, firemen and travellers); people splash water on them and pray for the souls of deceased ancestors.

The Gokusho 御供所 (offering hall, open daily 8.30am–5pm) is to the right before the bridge, with the Ajimi Jizo 嘗試地蔵 (tasting Jizo) beside it. This tasting Jizo is involved in a 1200-year-old ceremony called Shojin-gu in which priests serve Kobo Daishi meals (daily at 6am and 10.30am) after first offering some to the Jizo.

Cross the *gobyo-bashi* bridge 御廟橋 over the Tama-gawa River and enter the most sacred area. Try to pick up the Miroku-ishi stone 弥勒石 (LHS) with one hand. If it feels light you are good, and bad if it's heavy! Reach the Toro-do 燈籠堂 (Hall of Lanterns, open daily 6am–5.30pm), with over 10,000 lanterns hanging inside (two of which have been burning for almost 1000 years), and if you walk around to the back of the building you'll reach the Kobo Daishi Gobyo 弘法大師御廟 (mausoleum) where Kobo Daishi is said to be in eternal meditation.

Other sights in Koyasan include:
Daishi Kyokai Center 大師教会, a training centre for Buddhism in which you can participate in *shakyo* (sutra

A statue of Kobo Daishi (on the Choishimichi trail)

copying), and an *ojukai* ceremony where a priest recites the ten precepts of Buddhism.

Reihokan Museum 高野山霊宝館 contains over 28,000 cultural artefacts including national treasures and important cultural properties. Open May–Oct 8.30am–5.30pm, Nov–Apr 8.30am–5pm, modest entry fee, www.reihokan.or.jp (scroll down the home page for the English-language brochure).

Tokugawa Family Mausoleum 徳川家霊台 – constructed by Ieyasu's grandson Iemitsu (the third Tokugawa Shogun) in 1643 in a similar style to Nikko's Toshogu Shrine. You can see the mausoleum of the first Tokugawa

Shogun, Ieyasu (1543–1616) on the right and the second Tokugawa Shogun, Hidetada (1579–1632) on the left.

Kongosanmai-in Temple 金剛三昧院 – constructed at the request of Hojo Masako for the souls of her husband Minamoto Yoritomo (the first Shogun of the Kamakura Shogunate) and son.

There are a number of **hiking trails** around Koyasan: the Nyoninmichi 女人道 (maps available from the tourist office) is a good option for mountain views, with many options depending on time and fitness – the section between Fudozaka Nyonin-do to Daimon gate (around 1hr) is particularly recommended.

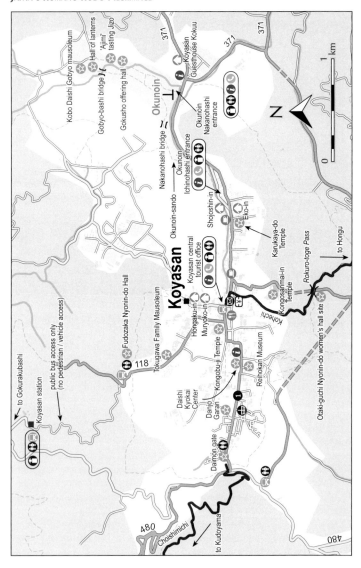

KOYASAN 高野山, 815M, POP 3300

Tourist office: Koyasan Shukubo Association 高野山宿坊協会 (temple-lodging booking and tourist office) has three locations with English-speaking staff, great maps, audio guides and bicycle rental. The central office 中央案内所 is in the main street near Senjuinbashi bus stop and the other two locations are opposite the Ichinohashi and Nakanohashi entrances to Okunoin, open daily 8.30am–5pm (Mar–Nov) or 9am–5pm (Dec–Feb), tel 0736-56-2616, http://eng.shukubo.net

Koyasan Visitor Information Center 高野山ビジターインフォメーションセンター (on the first floor of the Daishi Kyokai Center) has English-speaking staff and offers custom tours. Open daily except Tues & Thurs 10am–4pm (Apr–Nov) or Wed & Fri 10am–4pm (Dec–Mar), tel 0736-56-2270, www.koyasan-ccn.com

Where to eat: if staying in a temple, opt for half-board so you can experience *shojin-ryori* (Buddhist vegetarian cuisine) for dinner and breakfast. There are numerous cafés in town open for lunch, but not many stay open for dinner. One restaurant that is open all day (until 8pm) is Komi Coffee 光海珈琲 offering various set meals and desserts, near bus stop (no. 10) Ichinohashiguchi 一の橋口. Restaurants open for lunch include Bon On Shya 梵恩舎, a fantastic vegetarian café on the main road near bus stop (no. 7) Odawara-dori 小田原通. Maruman丸万 serves a multitude of Japanese dishes and has set menus at reasonable prices, next to bus stop (no. 15) Senjuinbashi W 千手院橋(西). Hanabishi 花菱, three doors down (east) from the post office, for those not on a budget. (Emperor and Empress Showa visited this restaurant in 1971 and 1977.) There are a few supermarkets, including the 24-hour Family Mart opposite the Danjo Garan complex.

Accommodation: Muryoko-in 無量光院 (tel 0736-56-2104, www.muryokoin.org, 25 rooms, ¥¥¥ incl D&B, founded over 1000 years ago, the older section of the building has rooms with beautifully painted sliding doors, closest bus stop: (no. 5) Koya Keisatsu-mae 警察前. Hongaku-in 本覚院 (tel 0736-56-2711, www.hongakuin.jp (Japanese site), 57 rooms, ¥¥¥¥ incl D&B. The Dalai Lama has stayed here and possibly admired the numerous gardens and painted screens by the famous Kano school in this welcoming and beautiful temple, opposite the police station, closest bus stop: (no. 5) Koya Keisatsu-mae 警察前. Eko-in 恵光院 (tel 0736-56-2514, www.ekoin.jp/en/index.html, 37 rooms, ¥¥¥¥ incl D&B. The monks from this temple run night-tours of Okunoin, closest bus stop: (no. 9) Karukayado-mae 苅萱堂前. Shojoshin-in 清浄心院 (tel 0736-56-2006, www.shojoshinin.jp (Japanese site), 30 rooms, ¥¥¥¥ incl D&B, a beautiful temple right next to the *ichinohashi* bridge entrance of Okunoin cemetery. Closest bus stop: (no. 11) Okunoinguchi 奥の院口). **Koyasan Guesthouse Kokuu** 高野山ゲストハウス コクウ (tel 0736-26-7216, **www.koyasanguesthouse.com**, 11 rooms including capsule rooms, and private rooms, ¥. This is a good choice for those on a budget, located a 3min walk east along the main road from Okunoin's Nakanohashi entrance. Closest bus stop: (no. 14) Okunoin-mae 奥の院前).

Stone mausoleums of Matsudaira Hideyasu and his mother in Okunoin

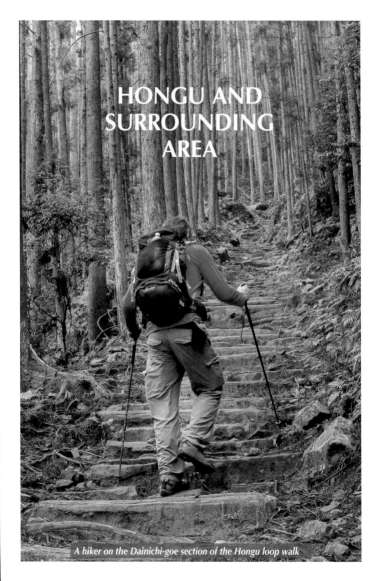

HONGU AND SURROUNDING AREA

A hiker on the Dainichi-goe section of the Hongu loop walk

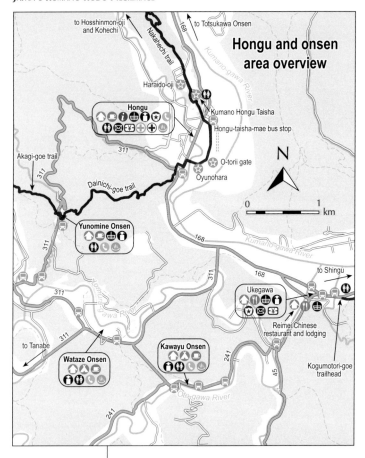

HONGU ONSEN AREA: YUNOMINE ONSEN 湯の峰温泉, 134M, POP 50

Discovered some 1800 years ago, Yunomine Onsen is thought to be one of Japan's oldest hot springs and is known for its healing properties. Traditional Japanese inns line both sides of the street in this diminutive village which

Yunomine Onsen

boasts three public *onsen*, including the World Heritage Tsuboyu Onsen. Intriguingly, there is also an *onsen* where you can boil eggs and vegetables.

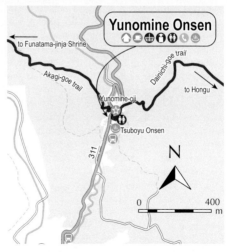

Yunomine Onsen

to Funatama-jinja Shrine

Akagi-goe trail

Dainichi-goe trail

Yunomine-oji

to Hongu

Tsuboyu Onsen

311

N

0   400
m

The legend of Oguri Hangan

Possibly the best-known story of Yunomine Onsen is the legend of Oguri Hangan and Princess Terute, often recounted in Kabuki plays (a style of traditional Japanese drama performed by men). Oguri fell in love with and married the princess, but her family couldn't accept the union and poisoned him. While Oguri went to hell, Terute was sent off to enslavement. After

91

some time, the god of hell sent Oguri back to the land of the living, but in a decrepit state; unable to walk, see, hear or talk. A monk hung a sign around his neck saying that he would be cured if taken to Yunomine Onsen to bathe in the healing waters and that anyone who helped would be blessed. Pulled along in a cart, including by an unknowing Princess Terute when he passed through her village, he eventually reached Yunomine Onsen. Upon bathing he was completely cured, and like in all good fairy tales, lived happily ever after with Princess Terute.

Access: serviced by buses from Hongu, Tanabe and Shingu, get off at Yunomine Onsen bus stop 湯の峰温泉 バス停 which is in the middle of the village. There is a detailed map at the bus stop including accommodation.

Visit: Tsuboyu Onsen つぼ湯 温泉 – a small hot spring bath (fits two people) in a wooden cabin in the creek. Thought to be named after its clay-pot shape, the water is said to change colour seven times a day. If you notice white specks in the water, they are naturally occurring mineral deposits, charmingly called *yu-no-hana* (hot spring flowers). Open daily 6am–9.30pm. Buy a ticket (¥770) from the vending machine opposite Toko-ji Temple, then exchange the ticket for a number at the adjacent kiosk. The number you receive represents your place in the queue and each party is allowed 30min. There is a waiting area outside the *onsen*; once it's your turn, take your shoes off outside and hang your number on the door. Soap and shampoo are not allowed. **Toko-ji Temple** 東光寺 – believed to be the initial source of the hot spring from a hole in the 'chest' of the enshrined Yakushi Nyorai statue (the Buddha of medicine and healing), the village's original name comes from this legend, with 'Yunomune' meaning 'chest of hot water'. **Yuzutsu** 湯筒 – the fenced-off cooking basin beside the creek (opposite Toko-ji Temple) where you can boil eggs and vegetables in the 90°C water. **Ippen Shonin stone inscription** 伝一遍上人名号碑 – Ippen Shonin (1239–1289), the wandering priest, reached enlightenment while spending 100 days in Hongu in 1274 then founded the Ji-shu school of Pure Land Buddhism. He established a religious dance and used this to teach his followers. It's also believed he carved this inscription (next to the Akagi-goe trailhead), which is a Buddhist prayer called the Nembutsu as well as the Buddhist Sanskrit letters, with his fingernail. **Yunomine-oji** 湯峯王子 – located a few minutes from Tsuboyu Onsen on the Dainichi-goe trail, this is one of the 99-*oji* (subsidiary shrines of the Kumano Sanzan).

Where to eat: Yunomune Jaya ゆのむね茶屋/湯胸茶屋, a teahouse serving breakfast and lunch, located next to Toko-ji Temple, open 7.30am–5pm. There is also a small restaurant/shop next to the *onsen* ticket counter and a small V-shop convenience store on the main road that sells snacks and eggs for boiling.

Accommodation: there are at least a dozen places to stay in Yunomine Onsen, ranging from hostels to top-end *ryokans*, including: J-Hoppers Kumano Yunomine Guesthouse ジェイホッパーズ熊野湯峰ゲストハウス (tel 0735-29-7666, http://yunomine.j-hoppers.com, eight rooms including bunk-bed dorms and private rooms, ¥+, shared kitchen, bathroom and communal areas – a great-value option in a terrific location). Minshuku Teruteya 民宿てるてや (www.teruteya.com (Japanese site), three rooms, ¥¥¥ incl D&B, named after Princess Terute of Oguri Hangan fame – a lovely guesthouse tucked away above the main road). Iseya Ryokan 伊せや (tel 0735-42-1126, www.yunomine-iseya.com (Japanese site), 14 rooms, ¥¥¥ incl D&B, in the middle of Yunomine Onsen next to the public bath and Toko-ji Temple). Yoshinoya Ryokan よしのや旅館 (www.yunomine.com/english.html, eight rooms, ¥¥¥¥, located just beyond Tsuboyu Onsen over a small footbridge, with a large *tanuki* (raccoon-dog) statue outside). Ryokan Adumaya 旅館あづまや (tel 0735-42-0012, www.adumaya.co.jp/english, 22 rooms, ¥¥¥¥¥. If you want to treat yourself to a special *onsen ryokan* experience, this is the place! The outstanding meals are made using *onsen* water and there are both indoor and outdoor *onsen*, some for private use).

HONGU ONSEN AREA: WATAZE ONSEN 渡瀬温泉, 83M, POP 98

Rotenburo *outdoor bath at Wataze Onsen*

A small village by the Yomura-gawa River, Wataze Onsen is the name of the area and Watarase Onsen is the name of the *onsen*/accommodation complex and also the name of the closest bus stop.

Access: serviced by buses from Hongu, Tanabe and Shingu; get off at Watarase Onsen bus stop 渡瀬温泉バス停 on Route 311, then go down the steps beside the bus stop.

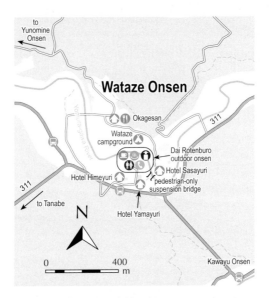

Visit: rotenburo outdoor onsen 大露天風呂 – the largest outdoor *onsen* in Western Japan, **www.watarase-onsen.jp**, open daily 6am–10pm, ¥700 for day guests (free if staying at one of the complex's three hotels).

Where to eat: there is a restaurant and souvenir shop inside the rotenburo complex, open 9am–7pm, and Okagesan おかげさん *yakitori* (skewered chicken) restaurant, a 7min walk following the road northwest from Hotel Sasayuri (open Tue–Sun 5pm–10pm).

Accommodation: there are three hotels within the Watarase Onsen complex, each with Western- and Japanese-style rooms and free access to the rotenburo outdoor bath, tel 0735-42-1185, **www.watarase-onsen.jp**: Hotel Himeyuri ホテルひめゆり (five rooms, ¥¥¥¥ incl D&B); Hotel Yamayuri ホテルやまゆり (19 rooms, ¥¥¥¥¥ incl D&B); Hotel Sasayuri ホテルささゆり (30 rooms, ¥¥¥¥¥ incl D&B). Guesthouse Okagesan ゲストハウスおかげさん (tel 0735-30-0681, **http://okagesankiitanabe.wixsite.com/kominkayado-okagesan** (Japanese site), a traditional Japanese house rental for up to eight people, ¥¥ (no meals), run by the owner of Okagesan *yakitori* restaurant, check-in at the restaurant).

HONGU ONSEN AREA: KAWAYU ONSEN 川湯温泉, 74M, POP 46

Fujiya Ryokan's river bath at Kawayu Onsen

By the Oto-gawa River, Kawayu Onsen (meaning 'hot water river') is known for its unique riverbed hot springs – dig a hole anywhere in the riverbed and hot water gushes out! During winter, a large open-air bath called Senninburo ('1000 people bath') is created in the river. There's a permanent riverbed bath on the other side of the suspension bridge with a pipe for cold river water if required.

Access: stretching for around 500m along the Oto-gawa River, Kawayu Onsen is serviced by buses from Hongu, Tanabe and Shingu. There are three bus stops: Kawayu Onsen 川湯温泉 バス停 at the western end, Kameya-mae かめや前 バス停 in the middle (in front of Kameya Ryokan) and Fujiya-mae ふじや前 バス停 (in front of Fujiya Ryokan).

Where to eat: there is one café, called Kobuchi こぶち, that serves lunchtime set meals, noodle dishes and rice balls, opposite Minshuku Kobuchi 民宿こぶち, open 11am–2pm.

Accommodation: Minshuku Omuraya 民宿大村屋 (tel 0735-42-1066, www. oomuraya.net (Japanese site), 20 rooms, ¥¥¥ incl D&B, with rooms overlooking the river and excellent meals, especially the lunch boxes. Bathing costumes

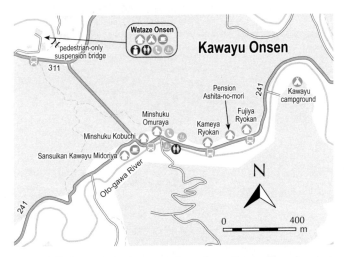

are available for use in the river *onsen*. Located near Kawayu Onsen bus stop).
Pension Ashita-no-mori ペンションあしたの森 (tel 0735-42-1525, **www. ashitanomori.jp/english**, six Western-style rooms, ¥¥¥ incl D&B, set in a Swiss-chalet-style log cabin, with Western-style meals served using local ingredients).
Kameya Ryokan 亀屋旅館 (**www.cameya.net/english.php**, 10 rooms, ¥¥¥¥ incl D&B, one of the oldest inns in Kawayu Onsen, it oozes tradition, located next to Kameya-mae bus stop). **Sansuikan Kawayu Midoriya** 山水館 川湯みどりや (tel 0735-42-1011, **www.kawayu-midoriya.jp** (Japanese site), 90 Western- and Japanese-style rooms, ¥¥¥¥¥ incl D&B, this multi-storey accommodation has an indoor *onsen* and two rock-pool baths built into the Oto-gawa River).
Fujiya Ryokan 冨士屋 (tel 0735-42-0007, **http://fuziya.co.jp/english**, 31 Western- and Japanese-style rooms, ¥¥¥¥¥ incl D&B, a popular high-end traditional *ryokan* with indoor and riverbed *onsen*, as well as superb meals, opposite Fujiya-mae bus stop).

ROUTE 1

*Hongu loop walk (including
Dainichi-goe and Akagi-goe)*

Start/Finish	Kumano Hongu Taisha 熊野本宮大社
Distance	16.7km
Ascent/Descent	875m
Difficulty	Moderate
Duration	8hr–8hr 30min
Access	Hongu: Hongu-taisha-mae bus stop 本宮大社前 バス停 is the closest to Kumano Hongu Taisha, and Kumano Hongu bus stop 熊野本宮 バス停 is the closest to the Dainichi-goe trailhead in Hongu. Yunomine Onsen: Yunomine Onsen bus stop 湯の峰温泉 バス停 is near the Dainichi-goe and Akagi-goe trailheads. Hosshinmon-oji: Hosshinmon-oji bus stop 発心門王子 バス停.
Waymarks	The Dainichi-goe trail 大日越 from Hongu to Yunomine Onsen has three waymarks counting up from 1 to 3. The Akagi-goe trail 赤木越 from Yunomine Onsen to Funatama-jinja Shrine has 11 waymarks counting down from 11 to 1. The Nakahechi trail 中辺路 from Funatama-jinja Shrine to Kumano Hongu Taisha has 17 waymarks counting up from 59 to 75.
Note	There are limited services so carry food and water and set out early to complete the loop.

This loop is made up of three trails of varying distances and difficulty and provides a perfect flavour of the Kumano Kodo. Allow a full day to walk the whole loop, including time to explore Yunomine Onsen. The loop or individual trails can be walked in either direction and are all well waymarked with bilingual signs. If you don't have your own hiking poles you may find wooden walking sticks provided in boxes at each trailhead.

The Dainichi-goe trail 大日越 (1.9km) between Hongu and Yunomine Onsen is a short but sometimes steep forest trail over Mt Dainichi. Allow around 1hr.

The Akagi-goe trail 赤木越 (5.7km) between Yunomine Onsen and Funatama-jinja Shrine has an initial steep ascent then an undulating forest trail before a final steep descent. The highpoint of the trail (alt 450m) between Akagi-goe waymarks 4 and 3 has mountain views. Allow 3hr–3hr 30min.

The Nakahechi trail 中辺路 (8.2km) between Funatama-jinja Shrine and Kumano Hongu Taisha is a relatively easy trail. If you have limited time, consider taking a bus to Hosshinmon-oji and walking to Hongu from there (7km). Allow around 3hr.

Starting at the base of the stairs to **Kumano Hongu Taisha**, cross the road (Route 168) and go down the small road opposite, following a wooden sign to 'Kumano Hongu Taisha Oyunohara'. Follow this narrow road around to the right and between rice paddies to Japan's largest *torii* gate, O-torii. You're now entering the original location of Kumano Hongu Taisha's shrine complex, called **Oyunohara** 大斎原. **350m**

Continue along the gravel road as far as the stamp box (RHS), then turn right and pass all that remains of

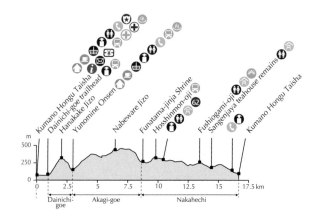

98

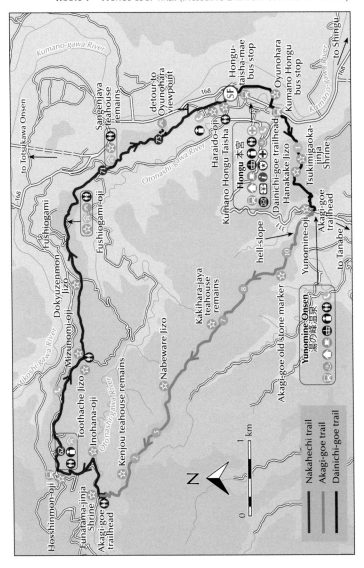

On the first day of Kumano Hongu Taisha's spring festival (13 April), young boys are carried over the Dainichi-goe trail on their father's shoulders.

the former shrine. Leave the grounds by turning right at the end, then go left and cross a small bridge over the Otonashi-gawa River. Go up the stairs and turn left onto Route 168. Take the next right then follow the road around to the left until the end, where you'll find **Kumano Hongu** bus stop 熊野本宮 バス停 and the **Dainichi-goe trailhead** 大日越登り口 (VM). ◄ **940m**

Go up the concrete staircase, following a wooden sign to 'Yunomine Onsen 湯の峰温泉' and pass in front of a few houses before ascending a stone staircase, climbing steeply into the cedar and cypress forest. After 500m pass **Dainichi-goe waymark 1** then after a further 100m reach **Tsukimigaoka-jinja Shrine** 月見ヶ丘神社. **1.5km**

Large cypress trees near Tsukimigaoka-jinja Shrine

Meaning 'moon-viewing hill', the god of agriculture and the sun goddess Amaterasu are enshrined in **Tsukimigaoka-jinja Shrine**. The shrine is surrounded by 300–400-year-old trees.

Turn right at the shrine and continue ascending to reach the highpoint of the Dainichi-goe trail at Dainichi-goe waymark 2 (alt 300m). Shortly after, reach a stone inscribed with the Nembutsu prayer (RHS, '南無阿弥陀仏' dating from 1342) near images carved into a rock called **Hanakake Jizo** 鼻欠け地蔵. ▸

Enjoy a brief section of level ground before starting to descend, steeply at times. After 700m and near the bottom, cross straight over an open grassy area then just before continuing down stone steps, **Yunomine-oji** 湯峯王子 (and the stamp) is a brief detour up to the right, signposted but easy to miss.

Continue downhill, soon passing a WC (RHS) opposite **Tsuboyu Onsen** つぼ湯 and cross the small bridge into the spa resort area of **Yunomine Onsen** 湯の峰温泉 (accommodation, café, supermarket, VM, WC – see 'Hongu onsen area: Yunomine Onsen' for details). **2.8km**

Hanakake Jizo, 'chipped nose Jizo', is associated with a local legend of a Jizo statue that protected an apprentice when his master thought he was selfishly eating his lunch.

Dainichi-goe trail near Hanakake Jizo

To continue the loop trail, turn right (or to visit Yunomine Onsen turn left). After 20m turn left up the stairs next to the sign for the Ippen Shonin stone inscription 伝一遍上人名号碑, at the **Akagi-goe trailhead** 赤木 越登り口. Start to ascend what's called '**hell-slope**' (so called because when pilgrims were travelling the opposite direction, they were descending this slope to the hot steam and sulphur smells of Yunomine Onsen) and after 850m near **Akagi-goe waymark 10**, look right for mountain views through the wire fence. A few minutes later pass a small **Akagi-goe stone marker** (LHS, dated 1855, with a finger pointing to Yunomine Onsen). Continue ascending and after a further 700m pass **Akagi-goe waymark 8**. **4.6km**

Akagi-goe stone marker (dated 1855)

The trail soon starts to descend, then shortly after passing **Akagi-goe waymark 7**, pass a small cemetery just before **Kakihara-jaya teahouse remains** 柿原茶屋跡 (RHS). Turn left and pass a statue of the Buddhist monk Kobo Daishi (LHS (774–835), the founder of Koyasan's Shingon Buddhist complex among many other things) and start uphill again for 1.1km to **Nabeware Jizo** 鍋割 地蔵. ▶ **6.3km**

Pass more mountain views then after a brief descent climb to the highpoint of the stage (alt 450m) shortly before **Akagi-goe waymark 3**. Continue as the trail undulates, then a few minutes after passing **Akagi-goe waymark 2**, pass the stone foundations of the **Kenjou teahouse** 献上茶屋跡 (no signpost) then turn right following signs to Funatama-jinja and descend, steeply at times. After 900m cross a log bridge over the Otonashi-gawa River, then turn right. Pass a WC (LHS, women: 女子便所, men: 男子便所) then a wooden pavilion housing an old river boat (the nearby Funatama-jinja Shrine is associated with the legend of the first boat) before a red metal bridge at the **Akagi-goe trailhead** 赤木越登り口. **8.5km**

Turn right onto a gravel road, following signs to Hosshinmon-oji 発心門王子, now on the Nakahechi route, soon passing Nakahechi waymark 59 next to **Funatama-jinja Shrine** 船玉神社.

> **Funatama-jinja Shrine** is associated with the legend of the god Susanoo who built the first wooden boat nearby. Fishermen come here annually to celebrate on 3 May. Tamahime Inari-jinja Shrine is on the RHS, guarded by two foxes.

After 300m turn right, down a forest path to reach **Inohana-oji** 猪鼻王子 then follow the path to reconnect with the gravel road and turn right. Shortly after, turn right up a stone staircase and after 400m go through a wooden *torii* gate to reach a paved road at **Hosshinmon-oji** 発心 門王子. **9.7km**

Nabeware Jizo means 'broken pot Jizo': legend has it a young disciple of Ippen Shonin was making rice here but ran out of water and the pot cracked as a result.

One of the five most important *oji*, **Hosshinmon** means 'gate of spiritual awakening', referring to a gate that once stood here marking the outer boundary of the sacred area.

Turn right, passing a stamp box and **Hosshinmon-oji** bus stop 発心門王子 バス停 then turn right onto a road, following a sign to Mizunomi-oji 水呑王子. Pass **Nakahechi waymark 62** and a rest shelter (WC), then VMs, and take the right fork onto a smaller road. Walk through a small settlement, passing rice paddies and fields, merging right at the end onto a larger road. Pass a payphone (LHS, accepts ¥10 and ¥100 coins), then take the right fork. After descending the small hill, pass the '**toothache Jizo**' 歯痛の地蔵さん (RHS, with a red bib, hiding behind a tree), then turn left and pass **Mizunomi-oji** 水呑王子 (WC), meaning 'drinking water' because of the adjacent spring. ◀ **11.4km**

Of the two Jizo statues here, the one on the RHS is broken in half and people hoping to heal their back pain place coins in the split.

Pass a white former school building and ascend a flagstone path into the forest. Shortly after passing a Jizo statue (called **Dokyuzenmon** 道休禅門の地蔵 placed here as a memorial for a monk who passed away), continue straight onto a road into the settlement of **Fushiogami** 伏拝, passing houses and rows of green tea shrubs. The locals often sell seasonal fruit, vegetables and honey along the road, with honesty boxes for payment. As the road bends right, continue straight up a dirt path, soon reaching **Fushiogami-oji** 伏拝王子 (WC, rest shelter, viewpoint). ◀ **13.4km**

Volunteers often serve delicious *onsen* coffee and refreshing *shiso* juice here; don't miss the viewpoint opposite the rest shelter.

Fushiogami-oji means 'kneel down and pray': this is where pilgrims have their first view of Hongu. Fushiogami-oji is also associated with the 10th-century female poet Izumi Shikibu: as a consequence of her pilgrimage, the Kumano region opened up to women.

Continuing on, after passing **Nakahechi waymark 71** cross the bridge over a road to **Sangenjaya tea-house remains** 三軒茶屋跡 (WC, rest shelter). This is the junction of the Nakahechi and Kohechi. There was once a *sekisho* checkpoint near here (see glossary) and three teahouses (*sangenjaya*). An Edo period stone marker remains, opposite the gate. **14.4km**

Continue through the replica wooden checkpoint gate '九鬼ケ口関所', uphill onto a pleasant section of trail. After 1km pass **Nakahechi waymark 73** then soon after, reach a side-loop trail (LHS) leading to a breath-taking **view** of Japan's largest *torii* gate in Hongu (highly recommended: to rejoin the trail from the viewpoint, descend along wooden steps, turning left at the end, then left again to rejoin the wide path of the Nakahechi 260m further along from where you left it). For the main trail, however, continue ahead and after a further 700m pass

A view of Oyunohara's O-torii gate, Hongu

The main street of Hongu

Meaning 'to exorcise', Haraido-oji is the last chance to exorcise your sins and purify yourself before reaching the shrine!

a **cemetery** (LHS) then join a road briefly before continuing straight down a stone staircase. Reach a road and continue downhill towards a VM and payphone (RHS), then pass Nakahechi waymark 75 and **Haraido-oji** 祓殿王子. ◀ Go through the opening in the hedge beside the back *torii* gate of Kumano Hongu Taisha 熊野本宮大社裏鳥居 (along the old path) and into the grounds of **Kumano Hongu Taisha** 熊野本宮大社 (WC). **16.5km**

See 'Kumano Hongu Taisha' for details on this and the surrounding area.

When leaving the shrine, the original Kumano Kodo route is parallel to the flag-lined stone steps, accessed just before the *temizuya* (water purification basin). The stage ends at the bottom of the stairs, where it began. **16.7km**

NAKAHECHI
中辺路

Early morning fog and mountain views in Takahara (Stage 1)

TANABE 田辺, 24M, POP 75,343

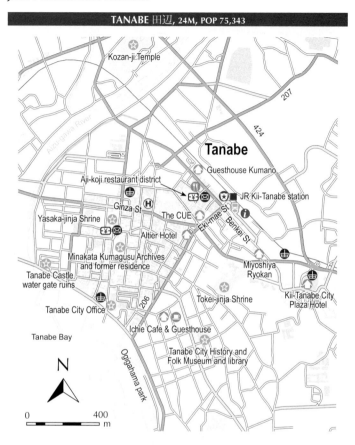

Tanabe is the second largest city in Wakayama Prefecture and is located in the southwest of the Kii Peninsula. Known as the 'gateway to Kumano', this is where the historic Kiiji route from Kyoto split into the Nakahechi and Ohechi routes to reach the Kumano Sanzan. Most people today take the 40min bus from Tanabe to the official starting point of the Nakahechi route at Takijiri-oji. During the Edo period (1603–1868), Tanabe became a castle

Aji-koji restaurant district, Tanabe

town and the ruins of the castle's water gate (田辺城水門跡) can be seen near the mouth of the Aizugawa River. Tanabe is the birthplace of the 12th-century warrior monk Musashibo Benkei, whose statue can be seen in front of Kii-Tanabe station. Often portrayed in traditional Kabuki and Noh dramas, Benkei is mentioned in the 14th-century novel *The Tale of the Heike*. Tanabe is also the birthplace of Ueshiba Morihei (1883–1969), the founder of the Japanese martial art Aikido.

Tourist office: the excellent Tanabe Tourist Information Center 田辺市熊野ツーリズムビューロー is next to Kii-Tanabe station and has English-speaking staff, maps, a superb detailed guide for the Nakahechi, bicycle rental and wi-fi. Open Mon–Fri 9am–5pm, tel 0739-26–9025, **www.tb-kumano.jp/en**. If you need to make any last-minute bookings when you arrive, they also run the nearby Kumano Travel, open daily 9am–6pm, tel 0739-22-2180, **www.kumano-travel.com/en**.

Visit: Tokei-jinja Shrine 闘鶏神社 – included in the World Heritage, the shrine dates to the fifth century. The name means 'cockfighting' and came about when local ruler Betto Tanzo picked sides in the Gempei War (1180–1185) by a cockfight between white roosters (the colour of the Genji clan) and red roosters (the colour of the Heike clan). The white roosters won, so he sent the Kumano fleet to support the Genji clan at the naval Battle of Dannoura (near present-day Shimonoseki). The Genji were victorious, leading to the establishment of the Kamakura Shogunate (1185–1333). **Ogigahama beach and park** 田辺扇ヶ浜海水浴場, a 15min walk from Kii-Tanabe station and a popular summertime bathing spot. **Kozan-ji Temple** 高山寺 – Kobo Daishi is believed to have visited before founding Koyasan and carved an image of himself for the temple after seeing his reflection in the river. There are shell mounds from the Jomon Era (around 10,000BC–300BC) with some pieces exhibited in the History and Folk Museum. The gravestones of Ueshiba Morihei and Minakata Kumagusu can be found here. **Minakata Kumagusu Former Residence and Archives** 南方熊楠顕彰館 – Minakata Kumagusu (1867–1941) was born in Wakayama and settled in Tanabe after travelling around the world. A botanist and conservationist among other things, Kumagusu is best known for his studies of slime-mould and being instrumental in saving many of the local shrines and forests by petitioning the government during the shrine-consolidation period that ran from 1906–1920. You can visit the house he lived in from 1916–1941, open Tue–Sun (closed every second and fourth Tuesday), 10am–5pm, ¥300.

Where to eat: Aji-koji 味光路 is the lively restaurant district a few minutes' walk from Kii-Tanabe station with over 200 establishments lining the narrow lanes. Pick up a city map from the tourist office for a list of restaurants and *izakayas* (Japanese-style pubs), many of which have English menus. Kanteki Izakaya かんてき oozes character (open 5pm–11pm, closed Wednesdays), Shinbe しんべ serves tasty shrimp croquettes '*ebi-koro* エビコロ' and set menus (open 5pm–10.30pm, closed Sundays) and Ginchiro Honten 銀ちろ本店 is a traditional-style Japanese restaurant with superb seafood, open 11am–10pm. There are cafés and shops selling *bento* lunchboxes near the station.

Accommodation: there's a wide range of places to stay in Tanabe, including business hotels, *ryokans*, rental houses and guesthouses such as The CUE (tel 0739-20-4297, **www.thecue.jp**, ¥, four private rooms with shared bathroom and kitchen in a terrific location, 3min walk from Kii-Tanabe station). Guesthouse Kumano ゲストハウス熊野 (tel 0739-34-2130, one male and one female Japanese-style dorm rooms located above the owner's restaurant, ¥, 3min walk from Kii-Tanabe station). Miyoshiya Ryokan 美吉屋旅館 (tel 0739-22-3448, **www.miyoshiya-ryokan.com/english**, 17 rooms some with en-suite bathrooms, ¥, 4min walk from the station and close to a Family Mart convenience store. The friendly and helpful owner, Ken, speaks English). Ichie Café (tel 0739-26-3239, two rooms with shared bathroom in a beautiful traditional house attached to the café, ¥¥, the welcoming owner serves delightful chiffon cake for breakfast, 10min walk from the station and 5min from Ogigahama beach). Altier Hotel アルティエホテル紀伊田辺 (tel 0739-81-1111, **www.altierhotel.com/english.html**, business hotel with 49 Western-style rooms, ¥¥, 5min walk from the station).

ROUTE 2

Nakahechi route

Start	Takijiri-oji
Finish	Kumano Nachi Taisha
Distance	63.8km
Ascent	3870m
Descent	3570m
Note	Detours as a result of weather-related damage are commonplace; always follow new signs where applicable.

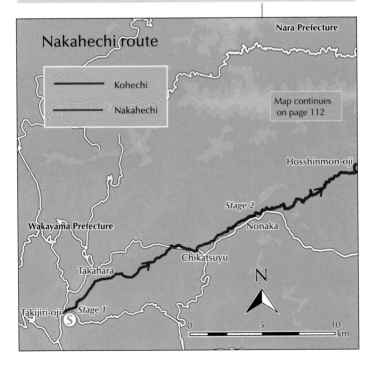

Map continues on page 112

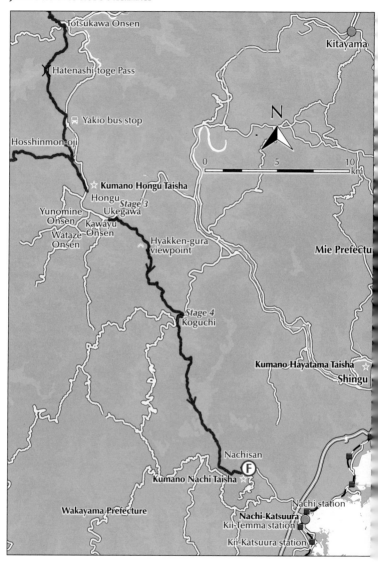

STAGE 1
Takijiri-oji to Nonaka

Start	Takijiri bus stop 滝尻 バス停
Finish	Tsugizakura-oji, Nonaka 継桜王子, 野中
Distance	16.4km
Ascent	1205m
Descent	765m
Difficulty	Moderate
Duration	8–9hr
Access	From Kii-Tanabe station: Ryujin or Meiko buses bound for Kumano Hongu Taisha depart from bus stop no. 2 at Kii-Tanabe station from around 6.25am, taking 40min. Get off at Takijiri bus stop on Route 31. Bus stops between Takijiri-oji and Tsugizakura-oji, bound for Hongu/Tanabe, include: 3.8km +2km Kurisu-gawa 栗栖川 バス停 (on Route 311, a 2km descent from Takahara rest area), 11.5km Gyuba-doji guchi 牛馬童子口 バス停 (on Route 311 next to the Michi-no-Eki Nakahechi road station), 13km Chikatsuyu-oji 近露王子 バス停 (Chikatsuyu has a number of bus stops), 16.4km +0.9km Nonaka Ipposugi 野中一方杉 バス停 (on Route 311, a 900m descent from Tsugizakura-oji).
Waymarks	Nakahechi 中辺路 wooden waymarks placed at 500m intervals from zero at Takijiri-oji to 33 (the last waymark before Tsugizakura-oji).
Note	Expect an average pace of 2–3km per hour owing to the terrain.

This stage is a perfect introduction to the Kumano Kodo – gnarly tree roots and rocks, flagstone paths, *oji* shrines, mountain views and verdant forest. The initial 4km up to the picturesque village of Takahara are, for many, the hardest of the stage. However, leaving Takahara the steep ascent continues as far as the highpoint at Uwadawa Jaya teahouse remains (alt 680m). From here, the trail descends to Chikatsuyu by the Hiki-gawa River, a popular accommodation choice. The final 3.5km to Tsugizakura-oji is mostly along the old highway and is a relatively easy few kilometres.

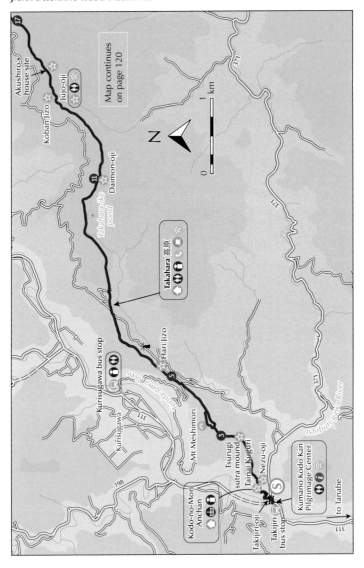

Map continues on page 120

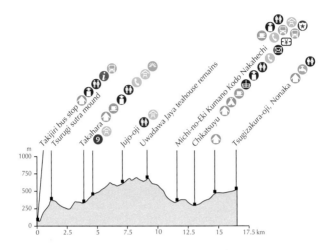

From **Takijiri** bus stop, cross the bridge over the Tonda-gawa River, and **Takijiri-oji** is on the LHS next to Kodo-no-Mori Anchan 古道の森あんちゃん (tel 0739-64-0929,

Takijiri-oji

five rooms, ¥¥ incl D&B, a convenient guesthouse with a shop that sells drinks/snacks/souvenirs, open daily 7am–5pm). Opposite is the **Kumano Kodo Kan Pilgrimage Center** 熊野古道館 (WC), an information centre and museum with a small selection of outdoor goods, open 8.30am–5pm.

> **Takijiri-oji** 滝尻王子, one of the 99-*oji* (subsidiary shrines), was also one of the five most important *oji* due to its location on the sacred Tonda-gawa River (a site for ritual water purification) and at the entrance to the Kumano region.

Tainai Kuguri means 'to pass through the womb'; in other words, be reborn. Women who make it through the cave are said to have an easy labour!

Facing Takijiri-oji, the wooden Nakahechi 'start' waymark is on the LHS of the grounds. Follow the path behind the shrine and begin ascending a stone staircase (next to the zelkova tree growing around a boulder), zigzagging uphill into the forest. After 350m, pass the **Tainai Kuguri** cave entrance 胎内くぐり. ◀ Try to squeeze through if you dare, or continue along the path, and around the corner pass Chichi-iwa rock 乳岩.

> **Chichi-iwa rock** is associated with the legend of Fujiwara Hidehira's (1122–1187) newborn baby which was left here and looked after by wolves. Hidehira is said to have donated a sword (*tsurugi*) to Takijiri-oji in thanks.

Meaning 'no sleep', Nezu-oji is thought to refer to the guards who had to stay awake to protect emperors and nobility.

Continue up a rocky path following Kumano Kodo signs, soon interspersed with intricate tree roots, and pass **Nezu-oji** 不寝王子. ◀ 580m

Nakahechi waymark 1 is shortly after on the RHS. Continue ascending, following signs to Takahara Kumano-jinja Shrine 高原熊野神社, and after 600m reach log seats and the **Tsurugi sutra mound** 剣ノ山経塚跡 (an ancient burial place for Buddhist sutras). Continuing on, a few minutes after passing **Nakahechi waymark 3** reach a short loop trail (up the steps next to a Japanese map) to **Mt Meshimori** 飯盛山 with fabulous mountain views. (From the top, the path continues downhill to rejoin the

Kumano Kodo after 270m.) Alternatively, keep right and descend for a further 700m, then go straight across a paved road and up the other side. There are a few log benches a few minutes after passing **Nakahechi waymark 5**, beside **Hari Jizo** 針地蔵. ▸ **2.7km**

Hari Jizo means 'needle Jizo': these three Jizos are said to heal toothaches.

Ascend steeply for 360m to a **TV tower**, then after a few more minutes continue onto a road, passing houses, then the **Iwami woodwork gallery** 岩見木工製作所. After a further 200m, on the RH corner, pass Takahara Kumano-jinja Shrine 高原熊野神社.

Takahara Kumano-jinja Shrine is believed to be the oldest shrine along the Nakahechi (circa 15th century). Don't miss the large camphor trees (*kusu-no-ki*; around 1000 years old), behind the shrine.

Just after this, reach a car park and viewpoint at **Kiri-no-Sato rest area** 高原霧の里休憩所 (VMs, WC, pay-phone, rest shelter) in **Takahara** 高原. **3.8km**

TAKAHARA 高原, 310M, POP 72

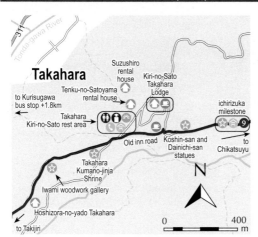

Known as the 'village in the mist', Takahara is a charming hillside settlement with terraced rice fields and glorious views of the Hatenashi mountain range; this is an ideal place to stay if you want to ease into the Kumano Kodo.

Access: the closest bus stop (Kurisugawa 栗栖川 バス停) is on Route 311, 2km downhill from the Takahara Kiri-no Sato rest area 高原霧の里休憩所.

Where to eat: Coffee Keyaki コーヒーけやき is a café with incredible mountain views on the trail just before leaving the village, open Fri–Mon 10am–5pm.

Accommodation: Kiri-no-Sato Takahara Organic Lodge 霧の郷たかはら (tel 0739-64-1900, www.kirinosato-takahara.com/en, eight (Western- and Japanese-style) rooms with panoramic mountain views, ¥¥¥ including D&B). Tenku-no-Satoyama 天空のさと山, Suzushiro すずしろ and Hoshizora-no-yado Takahara 星空の宿たかはら are rental homes bookable through www.kumano-travel.com/en

The trail continues opposite the rest area and soon you're ascending a narrow steep pavement, known as the '**old inn road** 旧旅籠通り', once lined with *hatago* inns 旧旅籠 for commoners. Almost at the top of the path, pass Coffee Keyaki コーヒーけやき (LHS with sweeping views and often a cute pony grazing), then turn right and left, back onto a forest path, passing a small shrine with two guardian statues, **Koshin and Dainichi** 庚申さんと大日さん (LHS). Begin the climb up to Jujo-toge Pass, ascending a flagstone path (*ishitatami* – see glossary) and just before Nakahechi waymark 9, pass a rest shelter and *ichirizuka* milestone 一里塚跡 (marking 24 *ri* – an old measurement of distance – from Wakayama Castle, around 94km). A further 700m uphill, pass **Takahara-ike pond** 高原池. ◀ **5.3km**

Still ascending, reach the remains of **Daimon-oji** 大門王子跡 next to Nakahechi waymark 11.

> **Daimon-oji** means 'large gate': there was once a gate here marking a boundary to the sacred area, as well as a rest area and drinking water according to diaries from the 12–13th centuries.

The path undulates for the next 1.4km before passing a rest shelter (RHS) just before a clearing with log

Perhaps a nice spot to compose a haiku (5-7-5 syllable poetry)!

A hiker on the trail near Daimon-oji

benches at **Jujo-oji** 十丈王子跡 (WC), Jujo-toge Pass 十
丈峠. ▶ **7.1km**

Pass the *oji* and Nakahechi waymark 14 and climb
steeply for 300m then pass **Koban Jizo** 小判地蔵 –
established by locals in 1854 after a pilgrim was found
deceased here with a *koban* (old coin) in his mouth. The
path undulates after **Akushiro's house site** 悪四郎屋敷跡,
then climbs steeply to reach the highpoint of the stage
at **Uwadawa Jaya teahouse remains** 上多和茶屋跡 (alt
680m). **9.1km**

Shortly after, pass Nakahechi waymark 18 and start
to descend, steeply at times for 800m before passing a
side-trail for the **Three-Fold Moon viewpoint** 三体月伝
説 (associated with a local legend; however, there's little to see from the viewpoint other than the sky). Take
the lower left path here, descending towards Osakamoto-
oji 大坂本王子, then after passing Nakahechi waymark
20, turn right onto a wider track and go straight across a

First referenced as
'Jyuten-oji' in 1201
when Emperor
Go-Toba visited,
this is a lovely spot
for a rest or lunch.

119

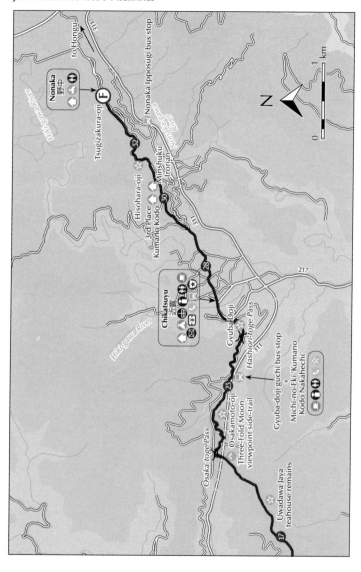

forest road (this is **Osaka-toge Pass** 逢坂峠), continuing steeply down a forest trail to **Osakamoto-oji** 大坂本王子跡, meaning 'base of a great slope': there's a 13th-century stone stupa here. (In spring it's possible to see the distinctive tubular Japanese Cobra Lily – *Arisaema yamatense* – in the area.) **10.8km**

Continue beside the stream, crossing it a number of times, then shortly after **Nakahechi waymark 23** when the trail meets Route 311, look right across the road and you'll see the **Michi-no-Eki Kumano Kodo Nakahechi road station** 道の駅熊野古道中辺路. ▶ Go up the stairs and turn right onto the old highway for 100m before rejoining a forest path (LHS). Continue uphill for 500m to **Hashiori-toge Pass** 箸折峠. **12.2km**

> Rest area with VMs, café, snacks, souvenirs, WC and payphone, open daily 8am–6.30pm. Gyuba Doji guchi bus stop is also here 牛馬童子口 バス停.

> **Hashiori** means 'break off chopsticks': one day when the young retired Emperor Kazan (968-1008) was on his pilgrimage after being overthrown, one of his assistants broke off a stalk of grass for him to use as chopsticks when they stopped here for lunch. When the stalk was torn, red liquid seeped out and the Emperor asked if it was blood ('chi') or dew ('ka tsuyu'), and so the area became known as 'Chi ka tsuyu'.
>
> There's a short side-trail here to the right leading to the **Gyuba Doji** 牛馬童子 site where there's a statue of former emperor Kazan riding a horse and cow, a statue of En no Gyoja, the seventh-century founder of Shugendo behind, and behind that, a 12th-century Hokyo-in stupa.

The trail descends, passing a popular cherry blossom area, rest shelter and the first views of Chikatsuyu in the valley. Reach the old highway and turn left, then after 50m turn right down a forest path. Just before reaching the road again, pass Cherry garden 'Sakura-no-Sono' 近露 櫻の園 (accommodation). Turn left onto the road then turn right and cross the bridge over the Hiki-gawa River 日置川, passing **Chikatsuyu-oji** 近露王子 (LHS) in **Chikatsuyu** 近露. **13km**

The Hiki-gawa River in Chikatsuyu

CHIKATSUYU 近露, 290M, POP 427

An old shop in Chikatsuyu's main street

The largest settlement of this stage, Chikatsuyu has ample facilities and is a popular place to overnight (although trying to find a room further along near Tsugizakura-oji is recommended to shorten the next stage). It was a post station in the Edo period (with 10 inns and 12

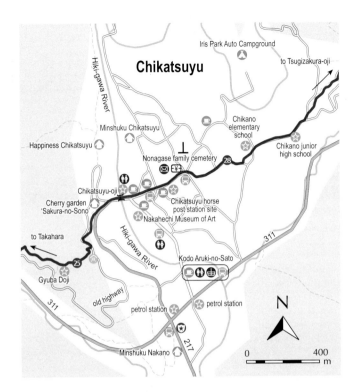

horses) and today facilities include accommodation, cafés, supermarket, post office/ATM and payphone.

Access: the village is serviced by a number of buses from Tanabe, Hongu and Shingu; the most convenient bus stops are Chikatsuyu-oji 近露王子 バス停 and Nakahechi Bijitsukan 中辺路美術館 バス停, next to the Nakahechi Museum of Art.

Visit: Kumano Kodo Nakahechi Museum of Art 熊野古道なかへち美術館, which includes work of the local-born artist Nonagase Banka (his house is just up the street along the Kumano Kodo where the Kotori-no-Ki café is) open Tue–Sun 10am–5pm, ¥250). The **Nonagase family cemetery** 野長瀬一族の墓, designated an important cultural asset. The family were allied with the Southern Imperial Court during Japan's Nambokucho war (1336–1392) and their stone stupa tombstones are thought to be around 500 years old.

Where to eat: around 500m from Chikatsuyu-oji is the Kodo Aruki-no-Sato 古道歩きの里ちかつゆ rest stop (on Route 311) with souvenir shops, an A Coop supermarket (open daily 8.30am–6pm) and restaurant. There are a number of cafés including Hashiori-chaya 箸折茶屋 next to Chikatsuyu-oji, open Tues–Sun 7am–5pm. Next door, Cabelo serves noteworthy coffee, open Wed–Sat 9am–5pm. Kotori-no-Ki 小鳥の樹 is inside the home of local artist Nonagase Banka, open Thur–Mon 10am–4pm (dinner available if booked in advance). Opposite the Nakahechi Museum of Art is Kissa Yumi 喫茶ユミ, open daily 8am–5pm, and Cafe Bocu カフェ朴 is just past the cemetery, open Wed–Sat 10am–4pm. Next to Chikatsuyu-oji bus stop there is also a local shop selling snacks with VMs outside.

Accommodation: Cherry garden 'Sakura-no-Sono' 近露 櫻の園 (**www.sakuranosono.online**, guesthouse rooms and a private rental house, ¥¥¥+ incl D&B, located on the Kumano Kodo at the entrance to Chikatsuyu). Minshuku Chikatsuyu 民宿ちかつゆ (tel 0739-65-0617, **www.ameblo.jp/chikatsuyu** (Japanese site), six rooms, ¥¥¥ incl D&B, located a short walk from Chikatsuyu-oji in a peaceful spot beside the Hiki-gawa River, with an *onsen*). Minshuku Nakano 民宿なかの (tel 0739-65-0317, five rooms, ¥¥ room only, shared kitchen, just across the other side of Route 311, 10min walk from Chikatsuyu-oji). Happiness Chikatsuyu ハピネスちかつゆ (a rental house for up to five people, ¥¥¥ incl D&B, located a short walk from Chikatsuyu-oji on the northwest side of the Hiki-gawa River).

Continue along the road through the centre of the village, passing the site of the Chikatsuyu horse post station 伝馬所跡 (RHS), just before the current post office, then continue straight, heading towards Hisohara-oji 比曽原王子. After passing **Nakahechi waymark 28**, turn left onto a paved footpath and pass **Chikano Elementary School** 近野小学校 (with a lovely lawn) then rejoin the road and keep right. Pass **Chikano Junior High School** 近野中学校 (RHS) then take the next left and soon after turn right onto a forest path. This lasts for 200m, then turn left onto a road and continue steeply uphill, passing **Nakahechi waymark 30. 14.6km**

Soon after, follow the road around to the right. (Or for 3rd Place Kumano Kodo 農家民宿さーどぷれいす熊野古道, turn left, +90m, tel 0739-65-0170, www.3rdplace-kumanokodo.com or www.kumano-travel.com/en, beautiful Japanese farmhouse rental, ¥¥¥ incl D&B.) Then, opposite glorious mountain views, pass Minshuku Irorian 民宿 いろり庵 (tel 0739-65-0105, two rooms, ¥¥¥ incl D&B, an evening shuttle service is provided to the nearby hot spring). After a further 450m pass **Hisohara-oji** remains 比曽原王子跡 (referenced in 1201 when Emperor Go-Toba visited), then at **Nakahechi way-mark 32** take the left fork following signs to Tsugizakura-oji. Shortly before reaching Tsugizakura-oji, pass the site of the **Nonaka horse post station** 野中伝馬所跡 (LHS, this one had 11 horses) then reach **Tsugizakura-oji** 継桜王子, Nonaka. **16.4km**

Toganoki-jaya teahouse next to Tsugizakura-oji

Thanks to the efforts of conservationist Minakata Kumagusu (1867–1941), the enormous **cedar trees** (*Nonaka-no-Ipposugi*; around 800 years old) in the grounds of Tsugizakura-oji were saved. Their one-directional branches face south towards Nachi, an auspicious direction believed to be that of Kannon's Fudaraku paradise. Tsugizakura means 'grafted cherry tree'.

NONAKA 野中, 517M, POP 183

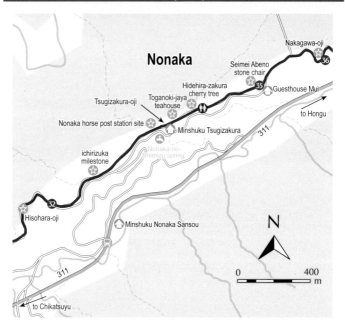

Almost halfway to Hongu, Nonaka is a picturesque area with (quite limited) accommodation, a WC (further up the road) and the Nonaka-no-Shimizu spring 野中の清水 (considered one of Japan's top 100 spring waters), a 2min walk downhill opposite Tsugizakura-oji. The quaint thatched-roof building next to the *oji* is called Toganoki-jaya とがの木茶屋 and is run by volunteers as a rest area with a traditional *irori* hearth inside.

Access: the nearest bus stop (Nonaka no Ipposugi 野中一方杉 バス停) is on Route 311, 900m downhill from Tsugizakura-oji.

Accommodation: Minshuku Tsugizakura 民宿つぎざくら (tel 0739-65-0009, three rooms, ¥¥¥ incl D&B, the owner is an ex-chef and a night here enjoying his incredible meals is sure to be a highlight of your trip. Access +50m: go down the road opposite Tsugizakura-oji and the Minshuku is on the LH corner). Guesthouse MUI ゲストハウス ムイ (tel 080-5682-2192, **www.guesthousemui. jimdo.com**, two rooms, ¥¥¥ incl D&B, with friendly hosts, a private bar and a few goats. Access +800m: continue along the trail and after passing Nakahechi waymark 35 opposite the 'Stone chair of Seimei Abeno', take the next right, doubling back along the road. The guesthouse is on the bend, RHS). Minshuku Nonaka Sansou 民宿のなか山荘 (tel 090-9093-7818, six rooms, ¥¥¥ incl D&B, located downhill on Route 311. Access +1km: go down the road opposite Tsugizakura-oji and turn right at Minshuku Tsugizakura. Soon after, turn left down the road opposite Nonaka-no-Shimizu spring. Reach an old temple and join a forest path behind the large bell, continuing downhill to a road and turn right. After a further 600m reach Route 311 (Nonaka no Ipposugi bus stop is to the right) and turn left; after a further 100m it's on the RHS).

Nonaka-no-Shimizu spring near Tsugizakura-oji

STAGE 2
Nonaka to Kumano Hongu Taisha

Start	Tsugizakura-oji, Nonaka 継桜王子, 野中
Finish	Kumano Hongu Taisha 熊野本宮大社
Distance	20.6km
Ascent	820m
Descent	1260m
Difficulty	Moderate
Duration	8–9hr
Access	The closest bus stop to Tsugizakura-oji is +0.9km Nonaka Ipposugi 野中一方杉 バス停 (on Route 311, a 900m descent from Tsugizakura-oji). Bus stops between Tsugizakura-oji and Hongu, bound for Hongu/Tanabe, include: 2.6km +380m Kobiro-oji guchi 小広王子口 バス停 (70m after passing Nakahechi waymark 39 turn right onto a road, doubling back and downhill for 380m to Route 311), 3.2km +400m Kobiro-toge 小広峠 バス停 (200m after Nakahechi waymark 40, follow a Kobiro-toge bus stop sign for 400m to route 311), 4.7km +600m Doyugawa-bashi 道湯川橋 バス停 (400m after starting the detour, instead of crossing the log bridge, continue down the paved road for 600m to Route 311), 13.6km Hosshinmon-oji 発心門王子 バス停, 20.6km Hongu-taisha-mae 本宮大社前 バス停 (in front of Kumano Hongu Taisha).
Waymarks	Nakahechi 中辺路 wooden waymarks placed at 500m intervals from 34 (soon after Tsugizakura-oji) to 75 (just before Kumano Hongu Taisha).
Note	This is a long stage with a hefty ascent and descent; if you'd like to shorten the stage, consider taking a bus to Kobiro-toge, Doyugawa-bashi or even Hosshinmon-oji.

The trail continues along the old Kumano Highway for 3km to Kobiro-oji remains (at Kobiro-toge Pass), then enters the forest and crosses three more mountain passes, reaching the highpoint of the stage at Iwagami-toge Pass (alt 671m). After crossing the last pass, Mikoshi-toge, it's almost all downhill, with one main exception up to Hosshinmon-oji. The remaining 7km passes through picturesque settlements and follows a wide forest trail to Kumano Hongu Taisha.

From **Tsugizakura-oji**, continue along the old high-way, passing the traditional thatched-roof building of **Toganoki-jaya** とがの木茶屋 then **Hidehira-zakura cherry tree** 秀衡桜. ▶ The Nakahechi now follows the old high-way for about 3km, passing **Nakagawa-oji** remains 中川王子跡 (LHS up a short side-trail), **Nakahechi waymark 37** then a rest shelter (LHS), and after a further 1.2km pass a few steps up to the left for **Kobiro-oji remains** 小広王子跡. **2.9km**

Shortly after, pass Nakahechi waymark 40 then turn right down a stone path into the forest at an overhead sign for the three spa areas (Yunomine, Kawayu and Wataze). This path soon meets the road again; turn right, passing a WC, then turn left doubling back down a gravel road and following a sign to Kumasegawa-oji. Cross a small bridge over the river then pass a rest shelter and begin to ascend a stone path through the forest, passing a Jizo statue (LHS).

Fujiwara Hidehira is said to have grafted a cherry tree onto a cypress here while praying for the safety of the baby he left behind in a cave near Takijiri-oji.

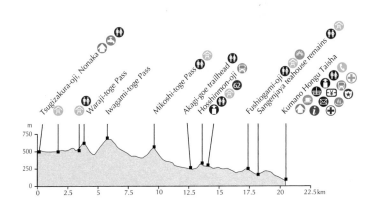

129

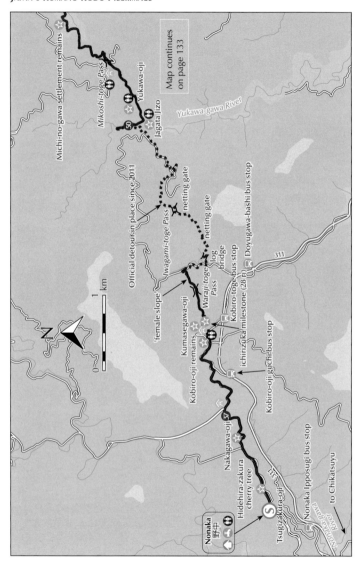

Map continues on page 133

Soon reach a fork (both options rejoin); if you turn left, you'll pass **Kumasegawa-oji** 熊瀬川王子 (first referenced by Fujiwara Yorisuke in 1210. After passing the *oji*, descend briefly then turn left to rejoin the trail). Or keep right at the fork, pass a small cemetery (RHS) then turn left, uphill. Either way, both routes converge then pass an **ichirizuka milestone** 一里塚跡 (marking 28 *ri* from Wakayama). Continue uphill for 350m to **Waraji-toge Pass** 草鞋峠. ▶ **3.9km**

Descend along the '**female slope**' (the 'male slope' is opposite in the landslide area not currently accessible) on a forest/flagstone trail for 400m, then turn right on a paved forest road following Kumano Kodo detour signs 熊野古道 迂回路 (a typhoon in 2011 damaged the trail). After 430m turn left down a few steps and cross a **log bridge** over the river then continue up the other side. Cross a quick succession of short log bridges then go through a **netting gate** and begin the long, steep ascent with gorgeous mountain views. After 640m go through a second **netting gate** and reach the highpoint of the stage at **Iwagami-toge Pass** 岩上峠 (alt 671m). **5.8km**

Meaning 'straw sandals pass', travellers often replaced their sandals at Waraji-toge before continuing.

Descending from Iwagami-toge Pass on the detour route

After catching your breath, begin to descend and after 900m reach a gravel forest road and turn left. After 700m fork right onto another gravel road, continuing downhill for a further 700m to reach the end of the detour. Turn right here, down a forest track leading to the Yukawa-gawa River 湯川川, shortly passing **Nakahechi waymark 50**. After about 250m reach a bridge across the river (with a wooden sign 'Yukawa-oji 0.4km'), but if you're collecting stamps, before crossing the bridge you'll want to turn right up the bank for 50m to reach **Jagata Jizo** 蛇形地蔵 (WC) – meaning 'snake-shape Jizo' because of the snake-like markings on the rock behind the statue. **8.5km**

Cross the bridge, then after passing **Yukawa-oji** 湯川王子 (WC, this was a popular place for pilgrims to stay overnight), begin to ascend the final pass for 750m to reach a paved road at **Mikoshi-toge Pass** 三越峠. ◄ Go through the wooden checkpoint gate 三越峠関所 then descend through the forest. After 1km the trail levels out briefly as you pass the **remains of Michi-no-gawa settlement** 道の川の集落. **10.7km**

There was once a teahouse and *sekisho* checkpoint here (see glossary); now there's a WC and rest shelter 20m to the left along the road.

A hiker on a lovely section of trail near Yukawa-oji

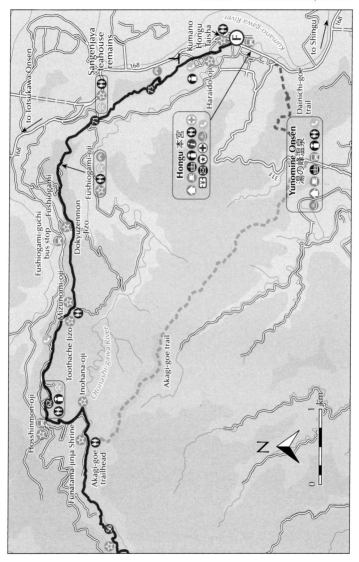

133

Michi-no-gawa was inhabited until the early 1970s and had 17 households in its heyday. The crumbling buildings and scattered homewares help to paint a picture of this old farming community.

Soon pass through a large clearing and landslide management area, before joining a gravel road. Pass **Nakahechi waymark 56** then after 270m turn right following a sign towards 'Inohana-oji', down stone steps to the Otonashi-gawa River 音無川. Follow the river for 1.1km, crossing it twice, then pass a red metal bridge at the **Akagi-goe trailhead** 赤木越登り口 (WC). ◄ **12.4km**

The Akagi-goe trail, popular since the 16th century, is the most direct way to Yunomine Onsen (+5.9km).

Continue along the gravel road towards Hosshinmon-oji 発心門王子, soon passing Nakahechi waymark 59 next to **Funatama-jinja Shrine** 船玉神社.

Funatama-jinja Shrine is associated with the legend of the god Susanoo who built the first wooden boat nearby. Fishermen come here annually to celebrate on 3 May. Tamahime Inari-jinja Shrine is on the RHS, guarded by two foxes.

After 300m turn right, down a forest path to reach **Inohana-oji** 猪鼻王子, then follow the path to reconnect with the gravel road and turn right. Shortly after, turn right up a stone staircase and after 400m go through a wooden *torii* gate to reach a paved road at **Hosshinmon-oji** 発心門王子. **13.6km**

One of the five most important *oji*, **Hosshinmon** means 'gate of spiritual awakening', referring to a gate that once stood here marking the outer boundary of the sacred area.

Turn right, passing a stamp box and **Hosshinmon-oji** bus stop 発心門王子 バス停, then turn right onto a road following a sign to Mizunomi-oji 水吞王子. Pass **Nakahechi waymark 62** and a rest shelter (WC), then VMs and take the right fork onto a smaller road. Walk through a small settlement, passing rice paddies and fields, merging right at the end onto a larger road. Pass a payphone (LHS, accepts ¥10 and ¥100 coins), then take the right fork. After descending the small hill, pass the 'Toothache Jizo' 歯痛の地蔵さん (RHS, hiding behind a tree with a red bib), then turn left and pass **Mizunomi-oji** 水呑王子 (WC), meaning 'drinking water' because of the adjacent spring. ▶ **15.3km**

Of the two Jizo statues here, the one on the RHS is broken in half and people hoping to heal their back pain place coins in the split.

Pass a white former school building and ascend a flagstone path into the forest. Shortly after passing a Jizo statue (called **Dokyuzenmon** 道休禅門の地蔵 placed here as a memorial for a monk who passed away) continue straight onto a road into the settlement of **Fushiogami** 伏拝, passing houses and rows of green tea shrubs. The locals often sell seasonal fruit, vegetables and honey along the road, with honesty boxes for payment. As the road bends right, continue straight up a dirt path, soon reaching **Fushiogami-oji** 伏拝王子 (WC, rest shelter, viewpoint). **17.3km**

> **Fushiogami-oji** means 'kneel down and pray': this is where pilgrims have their first view of Hongu. Fushiogami-oji is also associated with the 10th-century female poet Izumi Shikibu: as a consequence of her pilgrimage, the Kumano region opened up to women.

Volunteers often serve delicious *onsen* coffee and refreshing *shiso* juice here; don't miss the viewpoint opposite the rest shelter. Continuing on, after passing **Nakahechi waymark 71** cross the bridge over a road to **Sangenjaya teahouse remains** 三軒茶屋跡 (WC, rest shelter). ▶ **18.3km**

This is the junction of the Nakahechi and Kohechi. There was once a *sekisho* checkpoint near here and three teahouses (*sangenjaya*). An Edo period stone marker remains, opposite the gate.

Continue through the replica wooden checkpoint gate '九鬼ケ口関所' uphill onto a pleasant section of trail. After 1km pass **Nakahechi waymark 73**, then soon after, reach a side-loop-trail (LHS) leading to a breathtaking **viewpoint** of Japan's largest *torii* gate in Hongu (highly recommended: to rejoin the trail from the viewpoint, descend along wooden steps, turning left at the end, then left again to rejoin the wide path of the Nakahechi 260m

The entrance to Kumano Hongu Taisha

Meaning 'to exorcise', Haraido-oji is the last chance to exorcise your sins and purify yourself before reaching the shrine!

further along from where you left it). For the main trail, however, continue ahead and after a further 700m pass a **cemetery** (LHS) then join a road briefly before continuing straight down a stone staircase. Reach a road and continue downhill towards a VM and payphone (RHS), then pass Nakahechi waymark 75 and **Haraido-oji** 祓殿王子. ◄ Go through the opening in the hedge beside the back *torii* gate of Kumano Hongu Taisha 熊野本宮大社裏鳥居 (along the old path) and into the grounds of **Kumano Hongu Taisha** 熊野本宮大社 (WC). **20.4km**

See 'Kumano Hongu Taisha' for details on this and the surrounding area.

When leaving the shrine, the original Kumano Kodo route is parallel to the flag-lined stone steps, accessed just before the *temizuya* (water purification basin). The stage ends at the bottom of the stairs. **20.6km**

The following two stages of the Nakahechi (called the Kogumotori-goe and Ogumotori-goe) connect the Hongu area with Nachisan. The trailhead is in Ukegawa, 3km south of Hongu and is accessible by bus or walking.

STAGE 3

Kogumotori-goe route: Ukegawa to Koguchi

Start	Kogumotori-goe trailhead, Ukegawa 請川の小雲取越登り口
Finish	Koguchi village 小口
Distance	12.6km
Ascent	665m
Descent	650m
Difficulty	Easy
Duration	5–6hr
Access	The Ukegawa trailhead is accessible by bus from Hongu, the onsen areas and Shingu. The closest bus stop is Shimoji-bashi 下地橋 バス停, however, either of the Ukegawa 請川 bus stops (there are two, depending which direction you're coming from) are just a few minutes away. See Stage 4 for Koguchi access details. It's also possible to walk along the road (some sections without a pavement) from Hongu (3.3km), Kawayu Onsen (2.5km), Wataze Onsen (3.7km) or Yunomine Onsen (5.8km).
Waymarks	Nakahechi Kogumotori-goe 中辺路 小雲取越 wooden waymarks placed at 500m intervals count down to Nachisan from 54 (at the Ukegawa trailhead) to 30 (before leaving the forest path in Kowase).

Kogumotori 小雲取越 means 'passing over small clouds', referring to how high you climb. This is an easy hike as you gradually ascend a wide trail through lush forest, passing teahouse remains on the way to the highpoint at the spectacular Hyakken-gura viewpoint (alt 460m). The trail crosses a forest road then undulates en route to Sakura-toge Pass. The nearby Sakura-chaya teahouse remains is a nice spot for a break with a rest shelter and mountain views. Take care on the descent, which can be steep and slippery on flagstone.

The **Kogumotori-goe trailhead** 小雲取越登り口 on Route 168 is next to an information board, stamp, **Shimoji-bashi**

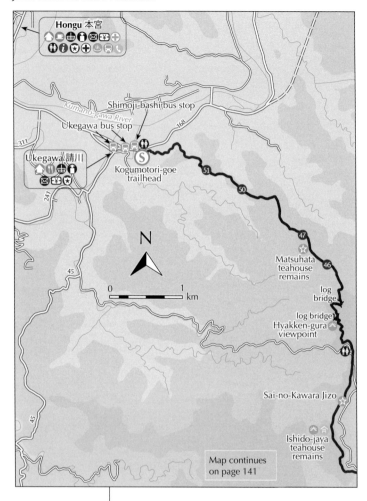

bus stop and the first/last Kogumotori-goe waymark 54. Go up the concrete steps between houses to reach a road then turn right, following signs to 'Koguchi 小口'. Continue uphill, past a bamboo grove (LHS) then pass

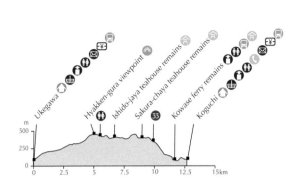

<table>
<tr><td>m</td></tr>
<tr><td>500</td></tr>
<tr><td>250</td></tr>
<tr><td>0</td></tr>
</table>

more houses and turn right up the stairs. Turn left at the top onto a grassy path and continue uphill into the cedar forest. After an initial steep ascent, the gradient becomes gentler along a wide, easy trail. Between **Kogumotori-goe waymarks 51** and **50**, keep left at the fork along the wide trail. Then after a further 1.6km pass **Kogumotori-goe**

Kogumotori-goe trailhead in Ukegawa

An easy section along the
Kogumotori-goe trail

This large flat area was once the location of four or five teahouses as recorded in diaries from the Edo period.

waymark 47 and go down stone steps to arrive at **Matsuhata teahouse remains** 松畑茶屋跡. ◀ **3.4km**

Continue to ascend, and immediately after passing **Kogumotori-goe waymark 46**, keep right at the fork following signs towards Koguchi 小口 (the left fork is for the Iseji trail via Banze-toge Pass). After crossing two **log**

Hyakken-gura viewpoint, Kogumotori-goe

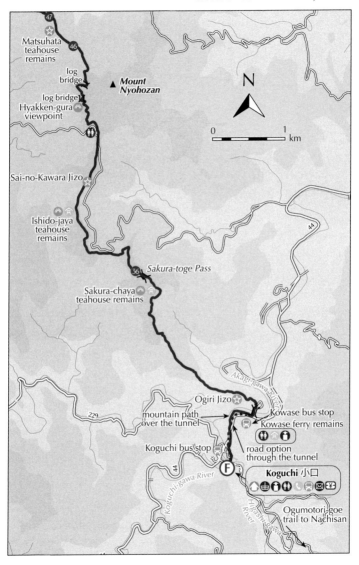

bridges and between Kogumotori-goe waymarks 44 and 43, reach the impressive **Hyakken-gura viewpoint** 百間ぐ ら (alt 460m) with a stunning view overlooking a sea of mountains called the '3600 peaks of Kumano'. **5km**

Descend for 800m to a road and continue straight across (or turn right for 150m to reach a WC). Then, just before Kogumotori-goe waymark 40, pass a statue on top of a cairn called **Sai-no-Kawara Jizo** 賽の河原地蔵.

> **Sai-no-Kawara** is the riverbed in the netherworld where Jizo helps the souls of deceased children pass into the afterlife. A local legend also claims this cairn was erected for a priest killed by wolves.

After a few more minutes reach **Ishido-jaya teahouse remains** 石堂茶屋跡 (rest shelter). **6.6km**

The path continues to undulate, then just before Kogumotori-goe waymark 37, start the last steep ascent and after 500m reach **Sakura-toge Pass** 桜峠 with a stone-engraved poem and **Kogumotori-goe waymark 36**. From here, begin a short, steep 500m descent to **Sakura-chaya teahouse remains** 桜茶屋跡 (rest shelter, viewpoint). ◀ **8.9km**

Named after the cherry tree that once stood in the garden of a teahouse here, this is a lovely rest area with mountain views.

Continue for around 800m before the final descent to the valley starts. Then, almost at the bottom and shortly before Kogumotori-goe waymark 30, pass **Ogiri Jizo** 尾切地蔵 (RHS) – a small shrine with two Buddhist statues, donated by locals in 1805 to protect travellers. Continue descending stone steps for a further 300m to reach a road and houses. Turn left then immediately right and go down a stone staircase to another road, then turn right and cross the **Kowase-bashi bridge** 小和瀬橋 to **Kowase ferry remains** 小和瀬渡し場跡 (VM, WC, rest shelter, Kowase bus stop 小和瀬 バス停). ◀ **11.7km**

Pilgrims would take a ferry across the Agaki-gawa River 赤木川 here before the bridge was constructed.

Turn right onto Route 44, then there are two options for the last kilometre to Koguchi. If you have the energy to go up and over the top of the tunnel on a forest path (100m longer, minimal waymarking): take the first right off Route 44, passing between houses with the river on the RHS. After 200m, just before the last house (LHS), turn left onto a gravel path and follow this as it becomes a flagstone path that climbs up and over the road tunnel, passing a Jizo statue and Koshin monument on top (RHS). While descending, continue onto a grassy path, passing a cemetery, and continue straight downhill until the path ends at a house, then weave right and left along a path between the houses and onto a driveway, downhill to the road. Continue straight along the road into the centre of **Koguchi**, passing the post office (RHS, with ATM), then Minakata Shoten supermarket (LHS) opposite a payphone and VMs. **12.6km**

KOGUCHI 小口, 60M

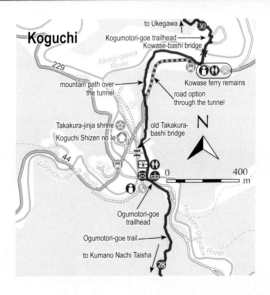

A small village with accommodation, a supermarket 南方商店 (open daily 7am–7pm), VMs, post office/ATM and a payphone (opposite the supermarket).

Visit: Takakura-jinja Shrine 高倉神社 (next to Shizen-no-Ie) – a designated cultural property and natural monument owing to the number of indigenous evergreen trees from the area growing in the grounds. Behind this shrine, on a small road across the river there's a rockface with 'Kumano stratum' ripple marks 化石漣痕 from when the area was on the seabed in the early Cenozoic period around 16 million years ago.

Accommodation: Koguchi Shizen-no-Ie 小口自然の家 (tel 0735-45-2434, **www.koguchi-house.info**, 11 rooms, ¥¥¥ incl D&B, the dining hall provides a great opportunity to meet fellow hikers in this converted school. Access: entering Koguchi from Kowase, turn right just before the post office and cross the old Takakura-bashi bridge 高倉橋. Go through the underpass and follow the road right then left to the accommodation).

Alternative route to Koguchi
Follow Route 44 and go straight through the road tunnel (100m shorter): after going through the tunnel, take the left fork and continue to the centre of Koguchi, passing the post office (RHS, with ATM), then Minakata Shoten supermarket (LHS) opposite a payphone and VMs. **12.5km**

Shizen-no-Ie accommodation in a converted school, Koguchi

STAGE 4

Ogumotori-goe route: Koguchi to Kumano Nachi Taisha

Start	Koguchi village 小口
Finish	Kumano Nachi Taisha 熊野那智大社
Distance	14.2km
Ascent	1180m
Descent	895m
Difficulty	Hard
Duration	7–8hr
Access	Koguchi is accessible by bus from Hongu or Shingu, although you need to transfer at Kanmaru 神丸. There are two bus stops in the area: Koguchi 小口 バス停 (closest to the Ogumotori-goe trailhead) and Kowase 小和瀬 バス停 next to the Kowase ferry remains and Kogumotori-goe trailhead.
Waymarks	Nakahechi Ogumotori-goe 中辺路 大雲取越 wooden and stone waymarks placed at 500m intervals count down from 29 (near the trailhead in Koguchi) to 1 (500m before Kumano Nachi Taisha).
Note	Carry food and water for the duration and allow plenty of time for this challenging stage.

This stage is infamous for being the most challenging of the Nakahechi as you gain 800m of elevation (Ogumotori 大雲取越 means 'passing over large clouds') along a steep, rocky and often moss-covered slippery trail, in addition to crossing three mountain passes. Consider this trail a lesson in concentration (watching every step)! There are four rest shelters en route; the shelter at Jizo-jaya teahouse remains makes a good lunch spot with a vending machine and WC, and the shelter at Funamichaya teahouse has the best views. The highpoint of the stage is the last mountain pass, Funami-toge (alt 883m) and the descent from there to Nachisan is dominated by rocks and flagstone paths (slippery when wet).

The Ogumotori-goe trailhead 大雲取越登り口 is at the end of the main street of **Koguchi**, just past the supermarket

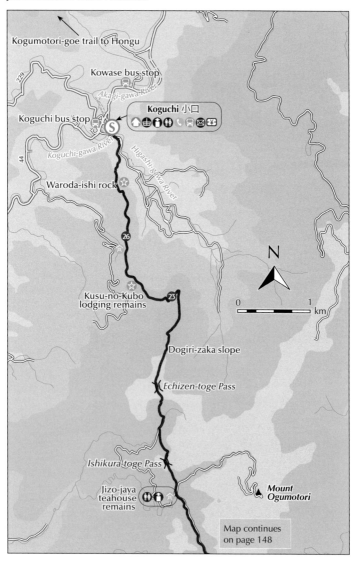

Kogumotori-goe trail to Hongu

Kowase bus stop

Akagi-gawa River

Koguchi 小口

Koguchi bus stop

Koguchi-gawa River

Higashi-gawa River

Waroda-ishi rock

26

Kusu-no-Kubo
lodging remains

23

Dogiri-zaka slope

Echizen-toge Pass

Ishikura-toge Pass

Jizo-jaya
teahouse
remains

N

0   1
km

▲ *Mount
Ogumotori*

Map continues
on page 148

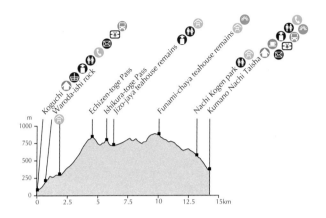

(open daily 7am–7pm). Go up a few steps and pass the stamp box (RHS), then a wooden Ogumotori-goe trail-head sign ('Kumano Nachi Taisha 14.3km') and continue uphill onto a forest path which soon becomes a road. Pass a couple of houses then keep right up the stone steps (following a Japanese sign towards Nachi: 那智方面 (大雲取越) へ) and after passing a few more houses, continue straight back onto a forest path and begin a steep ascent up stone steps. A few minutes after passing Ogumotori-goe waymark 28, reach **Waroda-ishi rock** 円座石. **750m**

> Thought to resemble a round cushion (*waroda*), **Waroda-ishi** is believed to be a meeting place of the three Kumano gods, represented in Sanskrit: Kannon, Yakushi Nyorai and Amida Buddha.

Continue ascending a flagstone path and shortly after passing **Ogumotori-goe waymark 26**, reach the first rest shelter. The ascent continues more steeply for 400m, then pass the **remains of Kusu-no-Kubo lodging** 楠ノ久保旅籠跡. ▶ **2.2km**

After passing **Ogumotori-goe waymark 23**, begin the **Dogiri-zaka slope** 胴切坂 (literally 'body-breaking

Records show there were at least 10 inns along this section of the trail during the Edo period.

slope'!) up a trail of stone, tree-root and wooden steps for 1.5km to reach the top at a stone-carved poem at **Echizen-toge Pass** 越前峠. **4.5km**

Descend from here for 500m to a stream, crossed on a concrete slab bridge, then soon begin to climb again for 500m to reach the next pass, **Ishikura-toge** 石倉峠 (there were once two teahouses here) with another stone-carved poem and a Jizo statue. Descend steeply along a stone path, passing the first of the Ogumotori-goe stone waymarks, 17. ◀ After a further 200m reach a gravel road and turn left, crossing the concrete slab bridge over the stream, then turn right onto a paved road and pass Jizo-ji Temple (LHS) just before **Jizo-jaya teahouse remains** 地蔵茶屋跡 (VM, WC, rest shelter). **6.2km**

Follow the road uphill beside the cascading stream (RHS), and a few minutes after passing **Ogumotori-goe waymark 14** turn right down a flagstone path, following signs to Nachisan 那智山. After 500m and three bridges, meet the road again and continue straight across, up

The remaining Ogumotori-goe waymarks are stone.

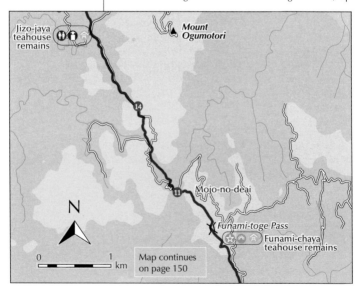

Map continues on page 150

A Jizo statue protecting hikers on the Ogumotori-goe

more stone steps. The trail goes downhill to a stream (RHS); after 700m reach the road again and turn left, immediately passing **Ogumotori-goe waymark 11**. As the road bends left, continue back into the forest along a flagstone path into an area called **Mojo-no-deai** 亡者 の出会い. ▶ After 800m reach the highpoint of the stage, marked by a small white Japanese sign, **Funami-toge Pass** 舟見峠 (alt 883m). **9.7km**

> **Funami-toge** means 'boat-viewing pass'. Nachi bay and Katsuura are straight ahead, with Shingu to the left, although the view is better from the teahouse remains coming up.

Just before starting to descend, pass a short side-trail leading left to **Funami-chaya teahouse remains** 舟見茶屋 跡 with a rest shelter and incredible Pacific Ocean views (not to be missed!). Begin the descent, and shortly before Ogumotori-goe waymark 5, pass **Noborite-chaya tea-house remains** 登立茶屋跡. ▶ **11.7km**

After descending for a further 1.4km, meet a road and turn right, then soon after, turn left at a large map (there's

Mojo-no-deai means 'encounter with the deceased'. Many pilgrims died on this arduous journey and there are a number of reports of their ghosts inhabiting the area.

Produce from Tanabe and seafood from Katsuura were sold at this teahouse, which had a reputation for healing people.

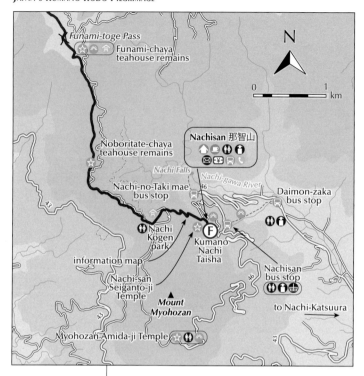

a WC 40m to the right) at the top of **Nachi Kogen park**
那智高原公園. Go down a grassy flagstone path through
the park, passing a rest shelter (LHS), then follow the
wooden 'Nachisan 那智山' signs straight across the road
to continue downhill. After 400m reach an **information
map** and turn left (**Myohozan Amida-ji Temple** 妙法山阿
弥陀寺 is to the right), then after 300m arrive at a paved
road at the end of the Ogumotori-goe trail. Turn right
and pass **Seiganto-ji Temple** 那智山青岸渡寺 (RHS) with
Nachi Falls views opposite, then walk through the orange
torii gate to enter the grounds of **Kumano Nachi Taisha** 熊
野那智大社. **14.2km**

See 'Kumano Nachi Taisha' for details.

KOYASAN 高野山 –
CHOISHIMICHI 町石道

Choishimichi stone marker

ROUTE 3
Choishimichi route

Start	Kudoyama station 九度山駅
Finish	Daimon Gate 大門, Koyasan 高野山
Distance	20.1km
Ascent	1145m
Descent	395m
Difficulty	Moderate
Duration	7hr 30min–8hr 30min
Access	This trail can be walked in either direction. Kudoyama is on the Nankai Koya line around 1hr 30min from Osaka. If walking downhill to Kudoyama station and you want to return to Koyasan: take the Nankai Koya line from Kudoyama to Gokurakubashi (30min), change onto the Nankai Koyasan cable car up to Koyasan station (5min), then take a bus into town.
Waymarks	Waymarks are limited before Jison-in Temple but then there are frequent green/yellow/white bilingual Choishimichi 町石道 signs.
Note	There are warnings for bears and hornets, so carry a bell as well as food and water for the stage.

The Choishimichi 'stone-marker path', constructed by Kobo Daishi from Jison-in Temple in the valley to the mountaintop Buddhist complex of Koyasan, is a long but rewarding hike with numerous historic sites en route. For the most part the trail is relatively easy underfoot, bar the odd rocky, slippery section. There are 180 *choishi* stone markers between Jison-in Temple and Koyasan's Danjo Garan, and carved onto each (in Japanese) is the marker number, Sanskrit name of the Buddha it represents, donor's name and date of construction (many from the 13th century). There are also four *ri-ishi* stone markers (old measurements of distance, placed at intervals of roughly 3.9km).

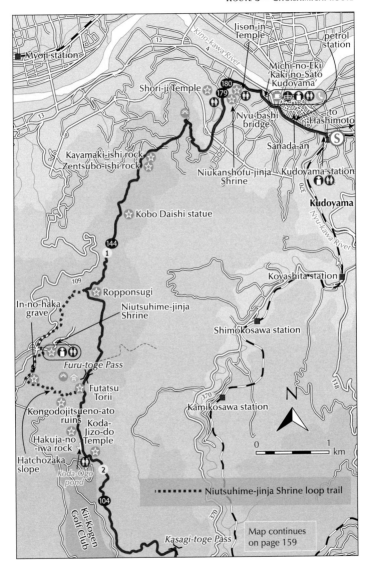

Myoji station

Jison-in Temple

petrol station

Kino-kawa River

13

Shori-ji Temple

Michi-no-Eki 'Kaki-no-Sato Kudoyama'

180
179

Nyu-bashi bridge

to Hashimoto

Kayamaki-ishi rock
Zentsubo-ishi rock

Sanada-an

Niukanshofu-jinja Shrine

Kudoyama station

Kobo Daishi statue

Kudoyama

Nyu-kawa River

144
1

Koyashita station

109

Ropponsugi

In-no-haka grave

Niutsuhime-jinja Shrine

Shimokosawa station

Furu-toge Pass

Futatsu Torii

Kongodojitsueno-ato ruins

Kamikosawa station

N

Koda-Jizo-do Temple

Hakuja-no-iwa rock

Hatchozaka slope

Koda-Oike pond

0   1 km

2

104

Kii-Kogen Golf Club

•••••••• Niutsuhime-jinja Shrine loop trail

Kasagi-toge Pass

370

Map continues on page 159

153

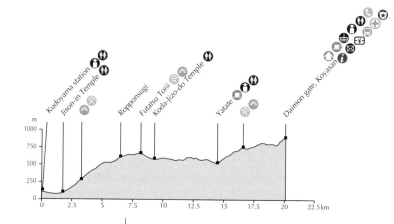

Kudoyama, meaning 'nine times mountain', refers to the number of times Kobo Daishi descended the mountain each month to visit his mother at Jison-in Temple (women were banned from entering Koyasan).

To visit Sanada-an Hermitage turn right here and continue for 100m..

Leave **Kudoyama** station and go down the steps next to the WC and **coin-lockers** then turn right and cross the pedestrian overpass. Now on Route 13, cross the bridge over the Nyu-kawa River 丹生川 and soon cross a second bridge, then after a further 250m pass a **petrol station** (RHS). ◄

SANADA-AN HERMITAGE 真田庵

Sanada-an Hermitage at Zenmyosho-in Temple, Kudoyama

Sanada-an Hermitage 真田庵 in Zenmyosho-in Temple 善名称院 (look for the gate with the six-coin family crest), enshrines three generations of the Sanada family warriors: Masayuki, Yukimura and Daisuke. During the Battle of Sekigahara (1600), the Daimyo feudal lord Sanada Masayuki (1547–1611) and his son Yukimura (1567–1615) were defeated by Tokugawa Ieyasu and sent into exile to Koyasan's Rengejo-in Temple. (It's possible to visit the room where they stayed at Rengejo-in Temple.) They were later allowed to move to Kudoyama to live with Yukimura's son and daughter-in-law. After 14 years, Yukimura saw an opportunity to take revenge against the Tokugawa army, but he and his son Daisuke were killed in their attempt during the summer siege of Osaka castle in 1615. Zenmyosho-in Temple was built in their honour in the 18th century on the site of their house. Masayuki's grave is in the grounds, open daily 7am–4pm. After an NHK TV drama series about the Sanadas was aired in 2016, a museum dedicated to the family opened. It is one block over from the temple and has costumes from the TV drama: Kudoyama Sanada Museum 九度山 真田ミュージアム, open Wed–Sun 9am–5pm, ¥500, www.kudoyama-kanko.jp/sanada (Japanese site).

Continuing on from the petrol station, reach a set of traffic lights and turn left to cross **Nyu-bashi bridge** 丹生橋. Continue straight on at the next lights, passing a playground (RHS), and you'll soon pass the back of **Michi-no-Eki Kaki-no-Sato Kudoyama** road station 道の駅柿の郷九度山 (RHS). ▶ Follow the road as it bends right, turning left just before the end (there's a small green sign), heading towards Jison-in Temple 慈尊院. Pass traditional houses and after 430m cross a short red bridge, now with the temple's stone wall on the LHS. Shortly after, turn left up the stairs and go through the wooden temple gate into **Jison-in Temple** 慈尊院 (WC). **1.7km**

Café, supermarket, VMs, WC, payphone, open daily 9am–6.30pm.

Founded by Kobo Daishi in 816 for his mother, **Jison-in Temple** became Koyasan's main administration office and winter base for the monks. Women visit for pregnancy, safe childbirth and recovery from breast cancer.

Go up the long stone staircase, passing the first *choishi* marker halfway up (RHS, 180 百八十町石), and into the grounds of **Niukanshofu-jinja Shrine** 丹生官省符神社.

Founded by Kobo Daishi in 816, **Niukanshofu-jinja Shrine** is dedicated to the local Shinto deity Kariba Myojin, who gave Kobo Daishi his two dogs to follow to Koyasan.

Turn right to leave the shrine, then left and pass *choishi* marker 179 (百七十九町石). Continue straight across the next road (**Shori-ji Temple** 勝利寺 and a WC are to the right) and keep right at the first small fork through a cemetery. At the second fork, keep left and uphill, passing a pond down below (RHS). Continue straight across the next two roads, following the winding path steeply uphill through a bamboo grove and persimmon and mandarin orchards for 800m to another road. (A 50m detour to the right here leads to a **viewpoint** (signposted 'tenbodai' 展望台) with picnic tables overlooking the Kino-kawa River.)

Veer left, continuing uphill, and after a further 900m (now on a forest trail), pass a sign pointing to the left for **Kayamaki-ishi rock** 榧蒔石, said to be where Kobo Daishi spread the seeds of the *kaya-no-ki* nutmeg tree so that the villagers could make a living by producing oil from the seeds. Soon after, pass a bench next to **Zentsubo-ishi rock** 銭壺石. ◀ **4.4km**

Meaning 'money-pot rock', a pot was once placed here with wages for workers and the opening was cleverly designed so each person could only retrieve the same amount of money.

Continue climbing the now rocky trail for around 600m before the path levels out, then after a further 250m pass a small seated **statue of Kobo Daishi** (LHS) holding prayer beads in his left hand and a *vajra* (a Buddhist ritual instrument) in his right. After 400m, pass *ri-ishi* marker 1 (一里石) next to **choishi marker 144** (百四十四町石) on the RHS. The trail begins to gently climb again, then after 800m reach the flat area of **Ropponsugi** 六本杉, meaning 'six cedars'. **6.5km**

There's a side-loop trail to Niutsuhime-jinja Shrine 丹生都比売神社 here, which is included in the World Heritage and worth the detour if you have the energy/time for an additional 1.2km.

Allow around 25min to descend (1.3km), visiting time, and 35min (1.5km) to climb up the Hatchozaka slope, rejoining the Choishimichi at Futatsu *torii*.

To visit Niutsuhime-jinja Shrine 丹生都比売神社

◀ Follow the 'Nyutsuhime-jinja Shrine 丹生都比売神社' sign onto the side-trail and descend for 1km to reach a paved road. Turn left, following 'Kinki Long Distance Nature Trail 近畿自然歩道' green/yellow/white signs. After 200m, turn left through the shrine car park, passing a WC (RHS), and go up the stairs then through the red *torii* gate. Cross the red arched Rinkyo bridge over Kagami-ike pond (mirror pond) and go through the middle *torii* gate.

Straight ahead is the 15th-century two-storey Romon gate with a cypress-bark roof. The **honden** (main shrine) is behind this gate, built in the Kasuga-style and the largest of its type in Japan. Also known as Amano Shrine, it was first referenced in 855 but is presumed much older. Enshrined are four deities including the two local Shinto gods who helped Kobo Daishi, Kariba Myojin and Niutsuhime. In the top left-hand corner of the grounds there is a collection of stone monuments including one honouring En-no-Gyoja, the founder of Shugendo.

The two-storey Romon gate at Niutsuhime-jinja Shrine, a side-trip off the Choishimichi

To rejoin the Choishimichi at Futatsu *torii* 二ツ鳥居, head back towards the middle *torii* gate and turn left, passing the shrine office 社務所 (LHS), then another WC (RHS). Turn left onto the small paved road and go uphill (there's a small sign towards 'Futatsu torii 二ツ鳥居'). Continue up the road for 380m then turn left at a bamboo grove with a green-and-white sign for Hatchozaka 八町坂 (the name of the slope). Shortly after, pass **In-no-haka grave** 院の墓 (LHS; originally thought to be the 12th-century grave of Emperor Toba's consort Taikenmon-in, it's now thought to be that of one of her maids, possibly the wife of the famous poet-monk Saigyo). Reach a small road, turn left and go uphill into the forest for 600m, then pass a sign for **Kongodojitsueno-ato ruins** 金剛童子杖の跡 (there is a slab of rock here believed to have holes from the walking staff of the Buddhist guardian Kongo Doji). Ascend for a further 300m before reaching a *torii* gate and junction; turn right to rejoin the Choishimichi (or left for a rest shelter and viewpoint) at **Futatsu torii** 二ツ鳥居.

For the main route from Ropponsugi 六本杉, turn left and continue along the now undulating trail. After 1.2km reach **Furu-toge Pass** 古峠 – there's no sign alluding to the pass but there's a side-trail on the left with a sign for 'Kamikosawa station 上古沢駅 2.5km'. After a further 400m reach a rest shelter and viewpoint (RHS, views overlooking Amano no Sato village 天野の里) next to two *torii* gates called **Futatsu torii** 二ツ鳥居. ◀

> The Niutsuhime-jinja Shrine side-trail rejoins the path here from the RHS.

> Originally built of wood by Kobo Daishi in 819 to represent the two local Shinto gods, Kariba-Myojin and Niutsuhime, the **torii gates** were reconstructed in stone in 1649.

Begin a gentle descent and after 500m pass **Hakuja-no-iwa rock** 白蛇の岩, meaning 'white-snake rock'. (If you see a white snake here it will supposedly bring you happiness.) **8.7km**

Continue downhill for 280m then pass Kii-Kogen Golf Club 紀伊高原ゴルフクラブ and **Koda-Ogo pond** 神

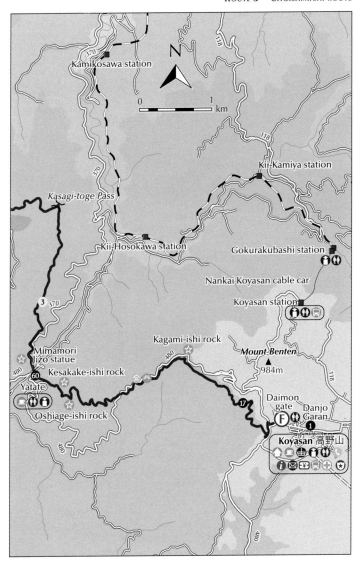

田応其池. After a few more minutes, pass **Koda-Jizo-do Temple** 神田地蔵堂 (there's a WC downhill opposite but be careful to step over the low electric fence that keeps wild boars out).

KODA-JIZO-DO TEMPLE

Koda-Jizo-do Temple features in the famous love story of Yokobue and Saito Tokiyori, retold in the 14th-century novel *The Tale of the Heike*. Yokobue, a lady-in-waiting to the empress, and Tokiyori, a high-ranking warrior, met and fell in love but Tokiyori's father forbade their union. Believing he could never love again, Tokiyori left and became a priest, but Yokobue found him in a temple in Kyoto. Tokiyori refused to meet her and moved to Koyasan, prompting Yokobue to become a nun, living out her final days in this nearby temple. Tokiyori, by this time an abbot of Daien-in Temple in Koyasan and known as Takiguchi, received word that Yokobue was living in Amano and was unwell. Soon after, while meditating in the garden at Daien-in, he heard the beautiful song of a nightingale. The singing suddenly stopped and when he looked he saw the nightingale had fallen from a plum tree into the well below and drowned; he knew Yokobue was dead. The pond, plum tree and memorials to Yokobue and Takiguchi can be seen in the garden of Koyasan's Daien-in Temple.

Yatate-chaya teahouse 矢立茶屋 sells grilled mochi rice cakes and a few snacks, open daily except Tuesdays, 9.30am–5pm.

Continue along the trail for 2.6km to a junction at **Kasagi-toge Pass** 笠木峠. (There is a side-trail here leading to Kamikosawa station 上古沢駅, +3.5km.) **11.8km**

Turn right and continue along the undulating path for 2.2km before passing the cute **statue of Mimamori Jizo** みまもり地蔵 (RHS, with a red bib and hat) then continue steeply downhill to reach Route 370 and **choishi marker 60** (六十町石) at a junction in **Yatate** 矢立 (café, VMs, WC). ◄ **14.5km**

Go up the small road to the left of the teahouse and continue uphill onto a forest path. After 400m pass **Kesakake-ishi rock** 袈裟掛石.

Kesakake-ishi rock is said to be where Kobo Daishi hung his stole, marking the boundary of the sacred area. It's believed if you can crawl through the gap you'll be gifted with a long life!

Soon after, pass **Oshiage-ishi rock** 押上石.

Oshiage-ishi means 'push-up rock', because when Kobo Daishi's mother tried to pass, a thunderstorm of fire erupted (because women weren't permitted) and Kobo Daishi lifted the rock to protect her.

After a further 1.4km, reach Route 480 and go straight across, up the forest path. After a few minutes pass a rest shelter and viewpoint (LHS), then after a few more minutes reach the road again, but don't cross; keep right along the forest path, heading downhill. After 1km pass **Kagami-ishi rock** 鏡石. ▸ **17.8km**

Kagami-ishi is known as the 'mirror rock' due to its flat shape. If you sit on the corner and recite mantras then your wishes will come true.

Cross a number of wooden bridges and continue the final ascent to reach Route 480 at the entrance to Koyasan at **Daimon gate** 大門 (WC). **20.2km**

To continue to *choishi* marker 1 (+600m), go through Daimon gate, passing *choishi* marker 6 (六町石) and a

One of the 180 choishi stone markers along the Choishimichi between Jison-in Temple and Daimon gate

Daimon gate, the main entrance to Koyasan

WC (LHS) then continue along the road. Shortly after passing the Family Mart convenience store (RHS), reach **choishi marker 1** (一町石) on the LHS, behind the wooden fence (with an English sign). The entrance to the **Danjo Garan** is on the left soon after this.

See 'Koyasan' for details of the spiritual complex and the town.

KOHECHI
小辺路

Descending through the forest from Hatenashi-toge Pass to Yakio bus stop (Stage 4)

ROUTE 4
Kohechi route

Start	Koyasan
Finish	Kumano Hongu Taisha
Distance	63.4km
Ascent	3245m
Descent	3880m

The Kohechi is a mountain trail recommended for experienced hikers, and preferably not undertaken solo or in bad weather. Each stage climbs to over 1000m and there are often sections of narrow, steep and rocky paths in areas prone to landslides. Note that detours are sometimes put in place to divert the trails around landslides; always follow new signs where applicable. Spring water, where mentioned, is not treated so you may wish to treat it if consuming. At each trailhead there are 'climbing notification boxes 登山届' with forms asking for your contact details, plan and emergency contact information. Even better would be to submit these details online: www.police.pref.nara.jp/cmsform/enquete.php?id=16

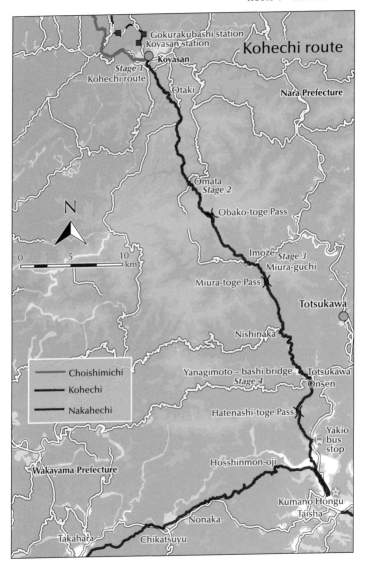

STAGE 1
Koyasan to Omata

Start	Koyasan central tourist office 高野山宿坊協会中央案内所
Finish	Omata bus stop 大股 バス停
Distance	16.8km
Ascent	660m
Descent	825m
Difficulty	Easy
Duration	5–6hr
Access	Koyasan: see 'Getting there', in the main introduction. Omata: there is very limited public transportation access (a community bus to Nosegawa village, then a Nankai Rinkan bus to Koyasan). If staying at Hotel Nosegawa, they can provide a free shuttle service to/from Koyasan (reserve at the time of booking).
Waymarks	There are 'Kumano Sankeimichi Kohechi 熊野参詣道 小辺路' bilingual wooden signs throughout the stage. (Kumano Sankeimichi means 'Kumano pilgrimage path'.)
Note	Carry food and water for the whole stage, and a ¥10 coin if you plan to call for a pick-up from your accommodation at Omata bus stop.

This is the 'easiest' stage of the four-day hike to Hongu, with significant sections of road. There is a very steep descent to the Odo-gawa River, followed by an even steeper climb! The forest paths are great underfoot and there are two rest shelters en route, one in the charming settlement of Otaki (5.8km) and the other along the Tainohara-sen forestry road with mountain views (11.6km).

See 'Koyasan' for details on the spiritual complex and town.

Starting from **Koyasan**'s central tourist office in the main street next to **Senjuinbashi east** bus stop, walk past the **fire station** 消防署 (LHS) and take the next right, passing a **Kongosanmai-in stone waymark** 金剛三昧院 on the

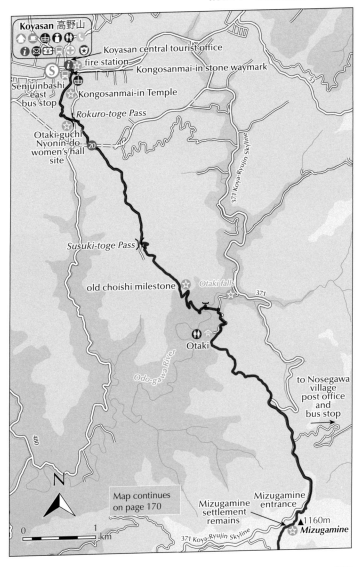

Koyasan 高野山

Koyasan central tourist office
fire station
Kongosanmai-in stone waymark
Senjuinbashi east bus stop
Kongosanmai-in Temple
Rokuro-toge Pass
Otaki-guchi Nyonin-do women's hall site
Susuki-toge Pass
old choishi milestone
Otaki falls
371
Otaki
Odo-gawa River
480
to Nosegawa village post office and bus stop
Map continues on page 170
N
0   1   km
Mizugamine settlement remains
Mizugamine entrance
▲1160m
Mizugamine
371 Koya-Ryujin Skyline
371 Koya-Ryujin Skyline
33

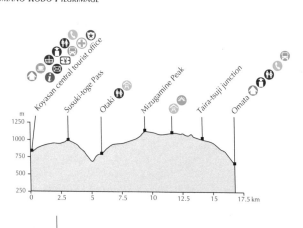

Hikers crossing the bridge over the Odo-gawa River (heading to Koyasan)

corner. Continue straight across the next street (there's a convenience store to the left) and take the next right at the entrance to **Kongosanmai-in Temple** 金剛三昧院, following 'Kumano Sankei-michi Kohechi' signs 熊野 参詣道小辺路. Continue up this road (which becomes gravel) for 700m to reach a small site with wooden signs (including Nyoninmichi 高野山女人道 waymark 18) and a stamp box at **Rokuro-toge Pass** 轆轤峠. **970m**

> Meaning 'long neck pass', Rokuro-toge Pass 轆轤峠 gets its name from the view women looked forward to seeing here on the **Nyoninmichi trail** – a trail that developed due to the ban (until 1872) on women entering Koyasan. There were seven trails up to Koyasan, and halls called Nyonin-do were built at the entrances marking the boundary for women to rest and worship at. The Nyoninmichi linked the halls, encircling the outer fringe of Koyasan. Otaki-guchi Nyonin-do women's hall was here, but today only one hall remains, at the Fudozaka entrance.

Continue uphill, joining the Nyoninmichi trail. After 450m, take the left fork at Nyoninmichi waymark 19, then soon after, leave the Nyoninmichi trail at **Nyoninmichi waymark 20** by continuing straight along the gravel forest road. After a further 1.7km keep an eye out for the wooden signs at **Susuki-toge Pass** 薄峠 ('Susuki-tohge' on the sign), meaning 'Japanese pampas grass'. **3.2km**

Turn left off the road here onto a forest path, following a sign towards 'Ohtaki 大滝', and descend into the valley. After 1.1km pass an **old choishi milestone** 丁石 (LHS). ▶ Continue steeply downhill for a further 600m before joining a paved road, and follow this down to the **Odo-gawa River** 御殿川. Cross the rusty red **bridge** then begin a ridiculously steep road climb. After 300m reach a wider paved road and turn right, continuing uphill. Soon pass a large shed (RHS) then after a further 370m pass a house (LHS) and take the left ramp uphill into the small settlement of **Otaki** 大滝 ('Ohtaki' on the sign), meaning 'large waterfall' after the nearby falls. **5.8km**

The engraving says '17 *ri* from Kumano Hongu'. A *ri* is an old measurement of distance, equivalent to about 3.9km, so this sign means about 66km from Hongu.

169

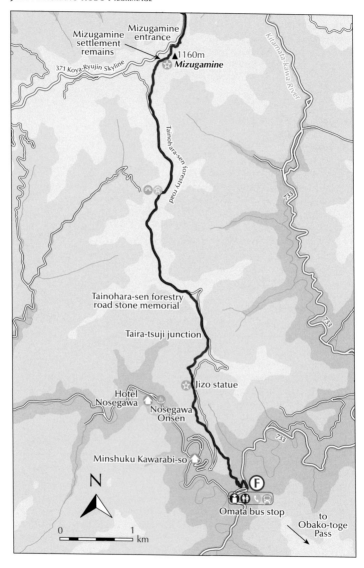

Rejoining a forest path at the Mizugamine entrance

Pass a picnic area with rest shelter and stamp box (RHS) – there is a WC opposite (behind the veggie patch in the brown hut) – then turn right, continuing up the road. After 300m pass the last house then rejoin a forest path and continue ascending. After 1.3km merge right onto the **Koya-Ryujin Skyline** highway 高野龍神スカイライン (Route 371). **7.4km**

Carefully follow the highway for 1.6km before turning left at the '**Mizugamine iriguchi entrance** 水ケ峰入口' with a colourful Japanese area map and wooden sign 'Omata 大股 7.7km'. The trail climbs steeply for 400m to the highpoint of the stage at **Mizugamine Peak and settlement** remains 水ケ峰集落跡 (alt 1160m). ▶ **9.4km**

Descend gradually along a forest path for 1km to meet the old paved **Tainohara-sen forestry road** 林道タイノ原線 and merge left, continuing a gradual descent with occasional views left of Mt Kojindake 荒神岳 (alt 1260m). After 1.1km, pass a rest shelter with mountain views (RHS). **11.6km**

Continue along the road for 1.5km then pass a **stone memorial** commemorating the opening of this forestry road (タイノ原線 林道開通記念碑) and very soon after, go

There was a popular inn here which was abandoned in 1952 after new roads were built: now there are just some remains of *ishigaki* stone walls (created to keep wild boar away from the crops), gravestones and a windbreak forest.

down a few steps on the RHS onto a forest path. After 300m, join the road again, then after a further 300m leave the road at the **Taira-tsuji junction** 平辻. (There are two Jizo statues behind a sign that says 'Omata 大股 2.9km'.) **14km**

Join the forest path here (RHS) and after 900m pass a **Jizo statue** (RHS), then after a further 600m rejoin the road. After a few more minutes reach another forest trail entrance and an information map (with sign 'Omata 大 股 1km') and turn left down the trail (to the left of the ascending wooden staircase). After 900m and a final steep descent, reach a road and turn right, then shortly after reach the end of the stage at the small wooden building (LHS) which is the **Omata** bus stop 大股 バス 停 (VM, WC, ¥10 payphone inside the wooden box). **16.8km**

OMATA 大股, 670M, POP 30

Kawarabi-so accommodation in Omata

The small settlement of Omata on the Kawarabi-gawa River 川 原樋川 has just a few houses across the bridge but no services other than what's here at the bus stop. Amago (red-spotted masu salmon) is a speciality of the area; if you enjoy fishing, enquire at your accommodation. The two accommodations listed, Minshuku Kawarabi-so (+1.6km/20min, RHS) and Hotel Nosegawa (+2.9km/40min, LHS) offer a pick-up service from here and you can call from the payphone. To walk to either, turn right along the road before the bridge and continue uphill, keeping the Kawarabi-gawa River on the LHS.

Accommodation: Minshuku Kawarabi-so 民宿かわらび荘 (tel 0747-38-0157, seven rooms, ¥¥¥ incl D&B, a friendly family-run *minshuku* (B&B) with delicious hot-pot dinners and transport to the nearby Nosegawa Onsen). Hotel Nosegawa ホテルのせ川 (tel 0747-38-0011, **www.hotel-nosegawa.jp/english**, 31 rooms, ¥¥¥ incl D&B, river-facing rooms and free access to the adjacent Nosegawa Onsen).

STAGE 2
Omata to Miura-guchi

Start	Omata bus stop 大股バス停
Finish	Miura-guchi bus stop 三浦口バス停
Distance	14km
Ascent	755m or 955m via Obako-dake summit
Descent	1020m or 1220m via Obako-dake summit
Difficulty	Moderate/hard
Duration	6–7hr
Access	Omata: see Stage 1 for access. Miura-guchi: there is a community bus (very limited schedule) to Totsukawa Onsen (transfer at Kawatsu 川津 heading towards Uenoji 上野地). Timetables (in Japanese): www.vill.totsukawa.lg.jp/life/transport/bus/pdf/kokudo2.pdf
Waymarks	There are 'Kumano Kodo Kohechi 史跡熊野参詣道小辺路' bilingual wooden signs and tall stone waymarks throughout the stage.
Note	There are no services during this stage so be sure to carry enough food and water. There is a payphone near the Obako-toge Pass trailhead; those who are staying at Minshuku Yamamoto and using their pick-up service can call from this phone.

This stage climbs up and over Obako-toge Pass (alt 1246m), and the summit (Obako-dake, alt 1344m; considered one of Japan's 'top 200 mountains') affords arguably the best Kohechi mountain views. After an initial very steep ascent out of Omata, the climb steadies into a comfortable, wide and generally obstacle-free trail. There's a WC and mountain hut at Obako-toge Pass, which, along with the summit or Uenishi's house, makes a good rest stop. Watch your footing as you descend an often steep and narrow trail and be mindful of landslides. There's a section of flagstone just before the Machidaira site, then a final steep descent to reach the trailhead in the small, almost forgotten village of Miura-guchi.

Starting from **Omata** bus stop, cross the bridge over the Kawarabi-gawa River 川原樋川 then begin climbing

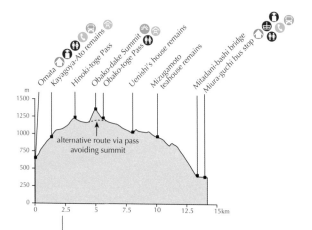

Omata
Kayagoya-Ato remains
Hinoki-toge Pass
Obako-dake Summit
Obako-toge Pass
Uenishi's house remains
Mizugamoto teahouse remains
Mitadani-bashi bridge
Miura-guchi bus stop

alternative route via pass
avoiding summit

Meaning 'thatch hut' there were once five houses here including a teahouse, barn (for cows) and fields for rice and crops. Today there's a basic log cabin.

steeply up the narrow road, passing houses. After a collection of **Jizo statues** and tombstones (RHS), continue steeply up the zigzagging forest path for 1km to the open space of **Kayagoya-Ato** remains 萱小屋跡. ◄ Continue ascending and after a further 2km reach a signpost marking **Hinoki-toge Pass** 桧峠. (Meaning 'cypress pass', legend has it Kobo Daishi threw away his chopsticks here and a cypress tree grew.) **3.2km**

Obako-dake summit

174

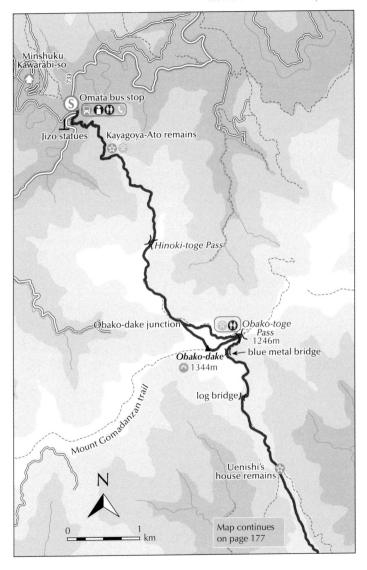

Minshuku
Kawarabi-so

Omata bus stop

Jizo statues

Kayagoya-Ato remains

Hinoki-toge Pass

Obako-dake junction

Obako-toge Pass
1246m

← blue metal bridge

Obako-dake
1344m

log bridge

Mount Gomadanzan trail

Uenishi's
house remains

N

0   1
         km

Map continues
on page 177

The path now undulates gently through a forest of beech and maple trees. After 1.4km, reach **Obako-dake junction** 伯母子岳分岐: keep left for the direct route to Obako-toge Pass 伯母子峠 (+1km; an easy stroll) or continue straight uphill for the summit **Obako-dake** 伯母子岳頂上 (600m away). (Right leads to Mt Goma-dan-zan 護摩壇山 in 12.7km – not included here.) From the summit (alt 1344m) there are views of the Omine mountain range to the east and Mt Goma-dan-zan to the west. You can continue from the summit down to the pass; follow the path left (with signs '帰り道') for 600m to arrive at **Obako-toge Pass** 伯母子峠 (alt 1246m). ◄ **5.5km**

Begin the descent near the WC, following stone and wooden signs to Uenishi's house 上西家跡 and Mitadanibashi bridge 三田谷橋. The first 1.5km is a gentle descent but with some very narrow cliffside sections; watch your footing. After the first 300m cross a short **blue metal bridge**, then after a further 900m cross a **log bridge**. After the path widens slightly, reach an area of an old landslide and a few sections with ropes in place, just before reaching the spacious open area and old stone foundations of **Uenishi's house remains** 旅籠 上西家跡. **8.1km**

A spacious level area with a basic hut (could sleep four to six) and WC.

The sign explains that according to a Kumano Guide (1682), a man called **Uenishi** owned an inn here and passing horsemen transporting rice and fish between Koyasan and Totsukawa would stop for tea. It was very lively in spring and summer when large numbers of pilgrims would stay overnight. Uenishi kept two cows and had a reputation for growing carrots and potatoes as good as those from Hokkaido.

Leave the site by going uphill, following new signs towards 'Miura-guchi bus stop 三浦口 バス停 6.7km'. After 300m reach the top and then begin to descend again, initially steeply, passing stone waymarks counting down the distance to Mitadani-bashi bridge 三田谷橋. After 1.6km reach a few log benches at **Mizugamoto teahouse remains** 水ケ元 (茶屋跡). **10km**

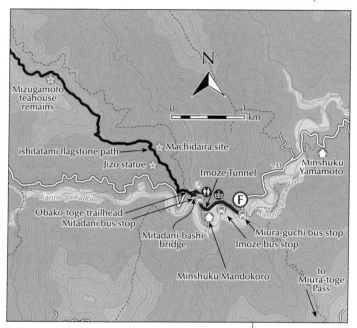

Mizugamoto means 'water source': Kobo Daishi (there's a statue of him here) is said to have founded a spring here which was known for its healing properties. The sign explains that according to legend, an old lady thought to be a *yamamba* (mountain witch) lived here, scaring anyone who saw her.

Continue descending through cedar forest and after 1km ascend briefly but steeply, reaching a wooden sign at the top for 'Miura Guchi bus stop 三浦口 バス 停 2.7km'. After a further 500m, descend along an **ishitatami flagstone path** intermittently for the next 500m to **Machidaira site** 待平 (松平). ▸ **12.1km**

After another 200m turn left at the stone marker 'Mitadanibashi bridge 0.9km' and **Jizo statue** (this Jizo is

According to a 17th-century Kumano guide, there was a house here; other reports say there was a teahouse and a *sekisho* checkpoint (see glossary).

177

*A directional
Jizo statue near
the Obako-toge
trailhead, Mitadani*

a directional waymark; the characters for 'left to Kumano'
are visible – '左くまの'). Descend steeply for 800m, passing another directional Jizo statue just before reaching a
paved road and the **Obako-toge trailhead** 伯母子峠登山
口. Turn left and cross the red **Mitadani-bashi bridge** 三
田谷橋, then after the bend, pass **Mitadani** bus stop 三田
谷 バス停 (RHS). Soon after, pass a WC and payphone
(LHS, in the wooden box, accepts ¥10 and ¥100 coins).
Continue along the road and through **Imoze tunnel**, then
for Minshuku Mandokoro 農家民宿政所 take the first
right (it's on the RH corner); otherwise continue ahead
and pass a local store called Fujiya 不二家 (LHS, limited

snacks). Shortly after, pass **Imoze** bus stop 五百瀬バス
停 and after a further 400m reach the end of this stage at
Miura-guchi bus stop 三浦口バス停 (RHS). **14km**

MIURA-GUCHI 三浦口, 360M, POP 30

An isolated hamlet deep in the mountains, there are a handful of houses,
one small local shop and a payphone near the Obako-toge Pass trailhead. At
the time of writing there was also a vending machine in front of a log cabin
near the Funato-bashi suspension bridge. At your accommodation, feast on
home-cooked delicious meals before stargazing – if you can stay awake late
enough!

Accommodation: Minshuku Mandokoro 農家民宿政所, (tel 0746-67-0476,
two rooms, ¥¥ incl D&B in a charming old farm house, run by the spritely
Mandokoro-san. Meals are prepared with produce from the garden. Located a
stone's throw from the local shop 'Fujiya'). Minshuku Yamamoto 農家民宿山本,
(tel 0746-67-0076, three rooms, ¥¥ incl D&B, this welcoming minshuku is 2.2km
from the Miura-guchi bus stop and the wonderful owners provide a pick-up service; call from the payphone near the Obako-toge Pass trailhead).

Bee hives full of character

STAGE 3
Miura-guchi to Yanagimoto-bashi suspension bridge

Start	Miura-guchi bus stop 三浦口バス停
Finish	Yanagimoto-bashi suspension bridge 柳本橋 (つり橋)
Alternative finish	Totsukawa Onsen
Distance	18.3km (+2km if visiting Totsukawa Onsen)
Ascent	780m
Descent	935m
Difficulty	Moderate
Duration	7–8hr
Access	Miura-guchi: see Stage 2 for access. Totsukawa Onsen: serviced by the Yagi–Shingu 'longest-mileage bus in Japan' (167km, 169 stops, 6hr 30min). The main bus stop, 'Totsukawa Onsen 十津川温泉 バス停', is in the centre of the village at the Totsukawa Bus Center 十津川バスセンター, www.narakotsu.co.jp/language/en. There are five daily services to Hongu (45min). The bus schedule can be downloaded from the Tanabe Tourist Information Center website, www.tb-kumano.jp/en (select 'Transport', 'Bus' and 'Timetables' and look for the Gojo–Shingu line). Nishinaka: there is a limited bus service between Totsukawa Onsen and the Miura-toge Pass trailhead in Nishinaka (two morning services and one afternoon). Enquire in advance from your accommodation, or timetables (in Japanese) can be found at www.vill.totsukawa.lg.jp/life/transport/bus
Waymarks	There are 'Kumano Kodo Kohechi 世界遺産 熊野古道小辺路' bilingual wooden signs and tall stone waymarks to Nishinaka 西中 on Route 425 (10.1km), then no waymarks to Totsukawa Onsen (but it's straightforward and described below).
Note	Once you descend from Miura-toge Pass to Nishinaka 西中, it's a further 8–10km road walk (depending on where you're staying) to Totsukawa Onsen 十津川温泉; allow 2hr–2hr 30min. Some accommodation providers offer a pick-up service and there's a payphone close to the Nishinaka trailhead. There is also an infrequent bus service to Totsukawa Onsen – see 'Access' above for details.

This stage crosses Miura-toge Pass (alt 1060m) with terrific mountain views looking back over the valley and Obako-toge Pass, and a number of historical sites en route. There are some sections prone to landslides, and watch your footing on the often steep and narrow sections. From Nishinaka it's an 8–10km road walk/bus/pick-up to the end of the stage, although any aches will be forgotten during a relaxing soak in the baths at Totsukawa Onsen!

From **Miura-guchi bus stop**, continue down the road, soon turning right opposite the old stone marker with a sign for 'Miura-toge Pass 三浦峠 4.5km'. Go downhill and cross the red **Funato-bashi suspension bridge** 船渡橋 then turn left, winding uphill, soon passing old rice terraces. After 400m follow the path right, passing between two houses then along a stone path. Shortly after, pass two wooden houses then enter the cedar forest and take the left fork uphill at the **stone marker** – 'Miura-toge Pass 三浦峠 3.1km'. After 300m pass enormous cedar trees just before the **remains of Yoshimura's house** 吉村家跡 防風林. **1.2km**

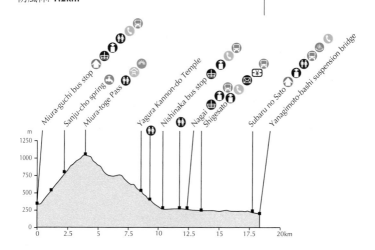

A hiker stands beside the enormous cedar trees near the remains of Yoshimura's house (photo: Howard Miller)

The site of a **former house and inn**, there were people living here until 1948. The large cedar trees are around 500 years old and are believed to have been planted to provide a windbreak.

You can just make out the numbers 二 十五 (25) carved on it. One *cho* is approximately 109m, so 25 *cho* is around 2.7km.

Continue uphill, and after 1km pass a small **choishi milestone (25)** 二十五丁石 (RHS). ◄ Then, after crossing the log steps with a handrail, reach a sign for Sanju-cho spring 三十丁の水 (just down to the right). Turn left, continuing uphill, and after a few minutes pass a **Jizo statue** and **choishi milestone (30)** 三十丁石 and continue climbing steadily, passing through landslide-prone areas and sections of blue netting to reach **Miura-toge Pass** 三浦峠 (alt 1060m) (WC, rest shelter). From the pass you

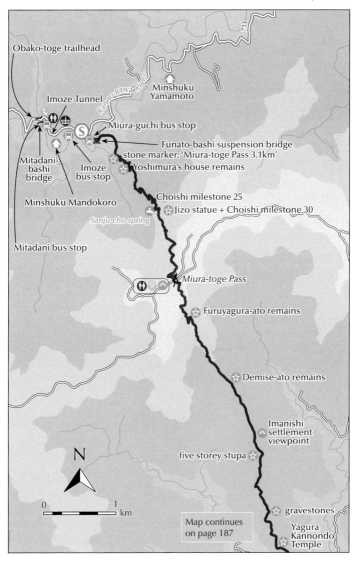

Obako-toge trailhead

Imoze Tunnel

Minshuku Yamamoto

Miura-guchi bus stop

Funato-bashi suspension bridge
stone marker: 'Miura-toge Pass 3.1km'
Yoshimura's house remains

Mitadani-bashi bridge

Imoze bus stop

Minshuku Mandokoro

Choishi milestone 25
Jizo statue + Choishi milestone 30

Sanju-cho spring

Mitadani bus stop

Miura-toge Pass

Furuyagura-ato remains

Demise-ato remains

Imanishi settlement viewpoint

five storey stupa

gravestones

Yagura Kannondo Temple

Map continues on page 187

N

0   1 km

183

Sections of netting just before Miura-toge Pass

can see Obako-dake and Miura-guchi down in the valley – with a zoom lens or binoculars you can even make out the Funato-bashi suspension bridge. **3.9km**

◀ To descend, go straight over the gravel forestry road onto a trail, following a white sign with red arrow (towards Nishinaka 西中). After 900m and a couple of wooden bridges, reach the **remains of Furuyagura-ato** 古矢倉跡. **4.8km**

The descent is often steep and narrow with more landslide-prone areas, so exercise caution.

> Deserted since 1935, Edo-period records describe a teahouse and inn here at **Furuyagura-ato**. There's a mossy Jizo statue (dated 1839) and a stone pillar in front engraved with the Buddhist Nembutsu prayer.

Continue downhill and after 850m reach the **remains of Demise-ato** 出店跡. ◀ Continue following the signs towards 'Kannondo 観音堂' with pleasant ridge sections (and **views** from the ridge of Imanishi settlement 今西集落 in the valley below, LHS) and after 1.3km, before the trail starts to descend again, pass a **five-storey stupa** 五輪の塔 (RHS). (It's easy to miss; look for the Japanese sign '五輪の塔' and the stupa is up a

There was once an inn, teahouse, and many rice paddies in the vicinity but the site has been deserted since 1910.

Follow this sign (towards Nishinaka 西中) to begin the descent from Miura-toge Pass

few metres behind this, surrounded by rocks. Each of its sections represents one of the five elements of earth, water, fire, wind and space.) **6.9km**

Start to descend again and after 1km pass some **gravestones** (LHS), then stone foundations, and after a further 600m reach a small temple called **Yagura Kannondo** 矢倉観音堂. ▶ **8.5km**

Continue downhill along some narrow and steep sections with safety rope; after 500m pass an **old wooden house** (LHS), then after a few more minutes reach a paved road with an information map and turn left (or turn right for a WC, +70m). Walk down the road for 240m, then turn right down a steep forest path for 300m before meeting the road again. Turn left, and after 60m go down the concrete stairs (RHS) to rejoin a forest path. Continue on this for 500m to reach the road one last time and a tall stone 'World Heritage' waymark at the **Miura-toge Pass trailhead** in Nishinaka 三浦峠登山口. **10.1km**

It's now an 8–10km road walk along Route 425 to the end of the stage (unless you've arranged a pick-up or are in time for the afternoon bus). Turn left along the road with the Nishi-gawa River 西川 on the RHS. Shortly after,

The three Buddhist statues inside are, from left to right, Jizo (dated 1725 and thought to cure earaches), a seated Nyoirin Kannon, and Kannon.

185

pass a green payphone (accepts ¥10/¥100 coins) next to a local shop (open daily 8am–4pm), then pass a VM and **Nishinaka** bus stop 西中 バス停. After 1.3km, pass a WC opposite **Kawai-jinja Shrine** 川合神社 then cross the bridge and keep right, with the Nishi-gawa River still on the RHS. After 400m continue straight and across another bridge into the village of **Nagai** 永井. **12.1km**

Pass Nagai bus stop 永井 バス停, opposite a VM and a local shop. After a further 1.2km enter the village of **Shigesato** 重里, passing Shigesato bus stop 重里 バス停 then a payphone (LHS) and Shigesato post office/ATM 重里郵便局 (LHS). As you leave the village, pass a VM (LHS). Continue along Route 425, passing more bus stops but no more facilities for 4.4km until you reach the large complex of **Subaru no Sato** 昴の郷 (accommodation, VM, WC, payphone). This complex includes the fancy Hotel Subaru ホテル昴 (tel 0746-64-1111, www.hotel-subaru.jp (Japanese site), 27 (Western- and Japanese-style) rooms, ¥¥¥¥ incl D&B, a luxury hotel in the Subaru-no-Sato complex with *onsen* pool and baths and incredible meals), Hoshi-no-Yu Onsen 星の湯, Subaru-no-Sato bus stop and the Yaen cable car 野猿. **17.9km**

If not staying at Hotel Subaru, continue along the road and just before the road tunnel, take the right fork. Go through an older tunnel then turn right at the end onto Route 735. After 70m reach the end of this stage at the **Yanagimoto-bashi suspension bridge** 柳本橋 (つり橋). **18.3km**

To visit Totsukawa Onsen (2km off-trail)

Cross the Yanagimoto-bashi suspension bridge over the Kamiyuno-kawa River 上湯川 and turn left onto a gravel path. Pass a house (RHS) then join a road. Ignore the concrete staircase (RHS; this takes you up to Hatenashi settlement) and continue down the road for 500m then cross the red road bridge (confusingly, this is also called **Yanagimoto-bashi bridge** 柳本橋). Turn right, now on Route 168, and after 160m pass **Warabio** bus stop 蕨尾 バス停. Continue along the road for 450m and after exiting from a tunnel, the first building on the RHS (with a

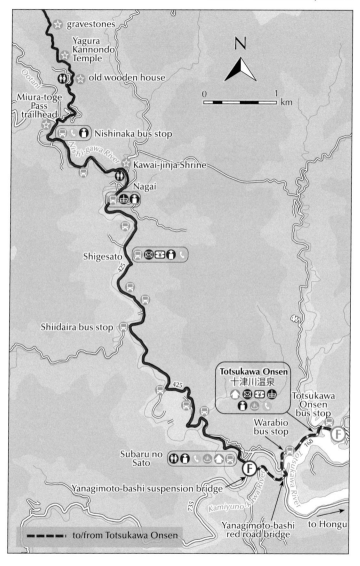

car park and VM) is Minshuku Yamatoya 民宿 やまとや. Continue along the road, then cross the bridge over the Totsukawa River into the centre of **Totsukawa Onsen**. Just after the bridge, pass Totsukawa Onsen **bus stop** 十津川温泉 バス停 (LHS, at the Totsukawa Bus Center 十津川バスセンター), then Fukuoka **supermarket** ふくおか next door (LHS), and opposite on the RH corner is Iori no Yu public *onsen* 庵の湯 (¥400, baths are made out of the local cedar).

TOTSUKAWA ONSEN 十津川温泉, 150M, POP 3488

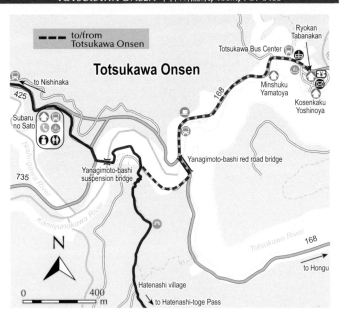

This *onsen* area, tucked away in the mountains of Nara Prefecture beside an emerald-green lake, is in Totsukawa village (Japan's largest village). It's believed the hot springs were discovered in the 17th century, and they are known for their healing properties.

Totsukawa Onsen

Visit: Iori no Yu 庵の湯 – public *onsen* in the centre of the village, with baths made from the local cedar, free foot and hand baths, as well as free *onsen* drinking water, open daily except Tuesdays 10am–9pm, ¥400. **Hoshi no Yu** 星の湯 – attached to Hotel Subaru, this *onsen* is open to the public (opening hours are longer for guests) and has indoor and outdoor baths, open daily midday–5pm, ¥800. **Yaen** 野猿 – meaning 'wild monkey', this is a traditional human-powered cable car used to cross the river (fits one person), located behind Hotel Subaru.

Where to eat: there are a handful of restaurants along Route 168, including one called 'Friends' (most only open for lunch), and Fukuoka supermarket ふくおか (open daily except Thursdays 7am–8pm) next to the Totsukawa Bus Center.

Accommodation: Minshuku Yamatoya 民宿 やまとや +1.6km (tel 0746-64-0028, www.yamatoya-totsukawa.com (Japanese site), ¥¥ incl D&B, tasty meals and a wonderful *onsen*). Ryokan Tabanakan 旅館 田花館 +1.9km (tel 0746-64-0014, www.tabanakan.jp (Japanese site), eight rooms, ¥¥¥ incl D&B, take the first right after the supermarket: it's the cream-coloured three-storey building on the bend (LHS)). Kosenkaku Yoshinoya 湖泉閣吉乃屋 (tel 0746-64-0012, www.t-yoshi-noya.jp (Japanese site), nine rooms, ¥¥¥¥ incl D&B, overlooking the river. Take the second right after the supermarket and it's at the end of the street overlooking the river (opposite the post office 平谷郵便局).

STAGE 4

*Yanagimoto-bashi suspension bridge
to Kumano Hongu Taisha*

Start	Yanagimoto-bashi suspension bridge 柳本橋 (つり橋)
Alternative start	Totsukawa Onsen 十津川温泉
Finish	Kumano Hongu Taisha 熊野本宮大社
Distance	14.3km (+2km if starting from Totsukawa Onsen)
Ascent	1050m
Descent	1100m
Difficulty	Hard
Duration	8–9hr
Access	Totsukawa Onsen: see Stage 3 for access. Yakio: there are buses to Hongu (10min), Shingu (1hr 30min) and Totsukawa Onsen (30min). The timetable can be downloaded from the Tanabe Tourist Information Center website: www.tb-kumano.jp/en (select 'Transport', 'Bus', 'Timetables' and look for the Gojo – Shingu line).
Waymarks	In addition to bilingual wooden and stone waymarks, there are 29 (of 33) Kannon statues 西国三十三観音 with numbered signs along the trail between Hatenashi village and Yakio. (The Kohechi doesn't pass Kannon statues 31 to 33 or 1.) There are no waymarks between Yakio trailhead and Sangenjaya teahouse (but the route is described below). From Sangenjaya teahouse remains, the Kohechi joins the Nakahechi 中辺路, passing Nakahechi waymarks 72 to 75 (placed at 500m intervals).

This stage crosses Hatenashi-toge Pass (alt 1060m), with a steep ascent and descent, sections of flagstone and natural forest. Passing through the small picturesque settlement of Hatenashi on the way up is a highlight, as are the views of Totsukawa Onsen near Kannon-do Temple, and of Hongu on the way down. Kannon statue 17 is at the pass. After descending steeply to Yakio bus stop, there's a 3km road walk to Sangenjaya teahouse remains, where the Kohechi joins the Nakahechi for the remaining 2km along a delightful forest path.

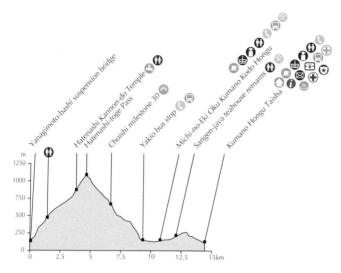

Yanagimoto-bashi suspension bridge

Hatenashi Kannon-do Temple
Hatenashi-toge Pass

Choishi milestone 30

Yakio bus stop

Michi-no-Eki Oku Kumano Kodo Hongu
Sangen-jaya teahouse remains

Kumano Hongu Taisha

Crossing the Yanagimoto-bashi suspension bridge over the Kamiyuno-kawa River at the beginning of the stage

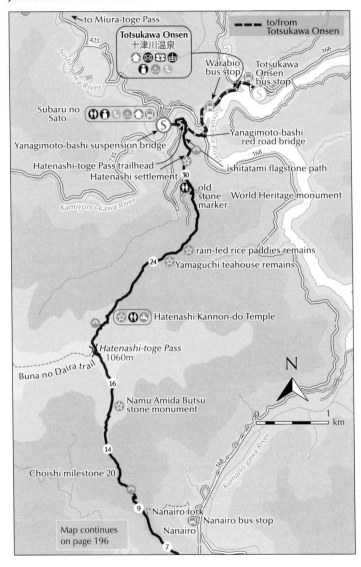

to Miura-toge Pass

to/from
Totsukawa Onsen

Nishi-kawa River

425

168

Totsukawa Onsen
十津川温泉

Warabio
bus stop

Totsukawa
Onsen
bus stop

Subaru no
Sato

Yanagimoto-bashi suspension bridge

Yanagimoto-bashi
red road bridge

Hatenashi-toge Pass trailhead

ishitatami flagstone path

Hatenashi settlement

30

old
stone
marker

World Heritage monument

Kamiyuno-kawa River

rain-fed rice paddies remains

24

Yamaguchi teahouse remains

Hatenashi Kannon-do Temple

Hatenashi-toge Pass
1060m

Buna no Daira trail

N

16

Namu Amida Butsu
stone monument

0   1 km

14

Choishi milestone 20

Kumano-gawa River

168

9

Nanairo fork

Nanairo bus stop

Map continues
on page 196

Nanairo

7

From Totsukawa Onsen

Retrace your steps back along Route 168 for 1km then cross the river on the red road bridge, **Yanagimoto-bashi** 柳本橋. Immediately turn right onto the small road and follow this for 350m (keep left when it forks) until you reach a Hatenashi-toge pass trailhead marker '果無峠 登山口' (LHS). Turn left and go up the wooden steps and onto the **ishitatami flagstone path** described below.

Cross the **Yanagimoto-bashi suspension bridge** over the Kamiyuno-kawa River 上湯川 and turn left onto a gravel path. Pass a house (RHS) then join a road briefly before continuing right, up a concrete staircase. Cross straight over a paved road with a **Hatenashi-toge pass trailhead** marker '果無峠 登山口' and go up the wooden steps and onto an **ishitatami flagstone path**. After 400m pass a **viewpoint** and bench, then a few minutes later go through a gate into the picturesque **Hatenashi settlement** 果無集落. (There's a stamp in a wooden box near the water trough.) ▶ **1km**

Called 'village in the sky', Hatenashi is one of 'Japan's top 100 villages', and it's easy to see why.

Hatenashi settlement

Pass through the settlement, go up the steps then pass the stone **World Heritage monument** (LHS) and continue straight across the road onto a path between houses. Go straight across the next road, up concrete steps, then pass **Kannon statue 30** 第三十番観音.

This mini **33 Kannon Pilgrimage** was installed by locals in 1922–23. The original pilgrimage, visiting 33 Kannon temples of Western Japan and called Saigoku Junrei, is Japan's oldest – it was founded in 718.

After 200m join a small road and pass between two houses; there's a WC on the RHS. Just before the next road, pass an **old stone marker** (LHS, inscribed with '左 やまみち' – left for mountain path and '右くまのみち' – right for Kumano). Reach the road and turn right, then turn left up stone steps at another trailhead entrance with a wooden sign 'Hatenashi-toge pass 果無峠 3.6km'. Continue uphill and after passing Kannon statue 25, reach a large open area that was once **rain-fed rice paddies** 天水田. **2.3km**

There are three Buddhist statues enshrined here, from left to right: the 11-faced Kannon, Sho-Kannon, and Fudo Myoo surrounded by flames.

After a further 300m, pass **Yamaguchi teahouse remains** 山口茶屋跡 (there are remnants of a stone wall and windbreaking cedar trees). Soon after, pass a Jizo statue next to **Kannon statue 24** (RHS) and continue climbing, steeply at times, along a delightful forest path for 1km before reaching **Hatenashi Kannon-do Temple** 果無観音堂 (spring water, WC). ◄ **3.7km**

Begin the final steep ascent, and after 300m (just before Kannon statue 19) pass a panoramic view (RHS) of Subaru no Sato, Hatenashi settlement and Totsukawa Onsen. After a further 600m reach **Hatenashi-toge Pass** 果無峠 (alt 1060m). **4.6km**

Enclosed within the forest there are a few log seats, the top half of a stupa and Kannon statue 17. There is also a side-trail here to Buna-no-Daira ブナの平; instead make sure to descend to the left towards Yakio 八木尾. The descent is at times steep and slippery with fallen leaves, stones and tree roots, so exercise caution.

Between **Kannon statue 16** and 15 pass the **Namu Amida Butsu stone monument** 六字名号碑 (the Nembutsu prayer), then after **Kannon statue 14** pass the round pebble-shaped **Choishi milestone 20** 二十丁石 (LHS). **6.2km**

The trail descends steeply to Kannon statue 12, then a few minutes later a stunning **view** towards Hongu and the Kumano-gawa River opens up. Continue descending, and after passing **Kannon statue 9**, take the right upper trail at the **Nanairo fork** 七色分岐 (the left is for Nanairo settlement 七色集落). The trail is easy-going along ridge sections between Kannon statue 8 and

Kannon statue 3

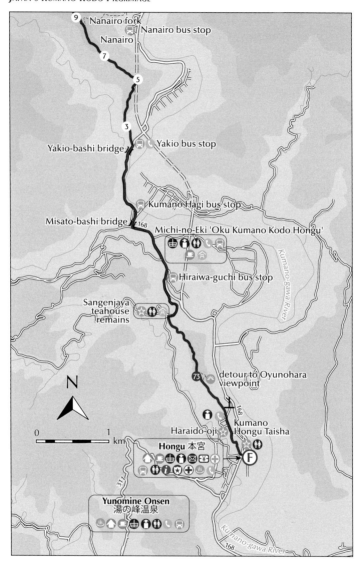

Kannon statue 5 (allowing your knees a short break), but take care to take the right fork after **Kannon statue 7** 第七番観音. **7.5km**

Descend steeply again after **Kannon statue 5**, passing a picnic table (RHS), then after **Kannon statue 3** continue straight and past a house (RHS). Just another 300m downhill through forest will bring you to the end of this mountain pass at **Yakio** bus stop 八木尾 バス停 (payphone). **9.2km**

To continue walking to Kumano Hongu Taisha 熊野本宮大社, turn right along Route 168 then cross **Yakio-bashi bridge** 八木尾橋 and continue along the road with the Kumano-gawa River 熊野川 on the LHS. After 900m pass **Kumano Hagi** bus stop 熊野萩 バス停 (LHS), then follow the road as it bends right, passing a barber shop in a log cabin (LHS). Cross the **Misato-bashi bridge** 三里橋 and turn left, then a few minutes later pass **Michi-no-Eki Oku Kumano Kodo Hongu** road station 道の駅奥熊野古道ほんぐう. ▶ **10.7km**

Continue straight along the road and after 600m pass a stone-carving workshop 野嶋石材店 (LHS) then soon after, take the right fork uphill at **Hiraiwa-guchi** bus stop 平岩口 バス停. After a further 600m follow a wooden sign 'Sangenjaya teahouse remains 三軒茶屋跡 +0.1km' onto the forest path (LHS), continuing uphill to the **remains** (WC, rest shelter). **12km**

> This is the **junction of the Nakahechi and Kohechi trails**; there was once a *sekisho* checkpoint near here and three teahouses (*sangenjaya*). An Edo-period stone marker remains, opposite the gate.

Turn left through the wooden checkpoint gate 九鬼ヶ口関所 now following a pleasant section of the Nakahechi route 中辺路 all the way to Hongu. After almost 1km, pass **Nakahechi waymark 73** then pass a side-loop trail (LHS) leading to a fantastic **viewpoint** of Japan's largest *torii* gate in Hongu (highly recommended: to rejoin the trail from the viewpoint, descend along wooden steps, turning left at the end, then left again

A fantastic rest area with café, supermarket, VMs, WC, payphone and bus stop, open daily 9am–6pm.

to rejoin the wide path of the Nakahechi 260m further along from where you left it).

For the main trail, however, continue ahead and after a further 700m, pass a **cemetery** (LHS) then join a road briefly before continuing straight down a stone staircase. Reach a road and continue downhill towards a VM and payphone (RHS), then pass Nakahechi waymark 75 and **Haraido-oji** 祓殿王子. ◄ Go through the opening in the hedge beside the back *torii* gate of Kumano Hongu Taisha 熊野本宮大社裏鳥居 (along the old path) and into the grounds of **Kumano Hongu Taisha** 熊野本宮大社 (WC). **14.3km**

See 'Kumano Hongu Taisha' for details on this and the surrounding area.

When leaving the shrine, the original Kumano Kodo route is parallel to the flag-lined stone steps, accessed just before the *temizuya* (water purification basin).

Meaning 'to exorcise', Haraido-oji is the last chance to exorcise your sins and purify yourself before reaching the shrine!

Monuments enshrining eight deities at Oyunohara

ISEJI HIGHLIGHTS
伊勢路

Flagstone and a stone slab bridge along the Iseji Magose-toge Pass trail

ROUTE 5
Magose-toge Pass 馬越峠

Start	Aiga station 相賀駅
Finish	Owase station 尾鷲駅
Distance	6.7km
Ascent	325m
Descent	335m
Difficulty	Moderate
Duration	3–4hr
Access	Train: Aiga 相賀駅 (+2.3km) is on the JR Kisei main line (one stop/6min from Owase 尾鷲, or 55min from Kumanoshi 熊野市, or 2hr 30min from Iseshi 伊勢市). Bus: Mie Kotsu buses bound for Matsusaka 松阪 or Kii-Nagashima station 紀伊長島駅 depart from Owase station (Owase-eki-guchi bus stop 尾鷲駅口 バス停) and stop at Washige bus stop 鷲毛 バス停, 12min, which is opposite the trailhead. Bus timetables (in Japanese) are available at www.sanco.co.jp
Waymarks	No waymarks from Aiga station to the trailhead, but then wooden bilingual 'Magose 馬越峠' waymarks placed at 100m intervals counting up from 1 to 22 over the pass, and limited waymarking in Owase.
Note	There are warnings of bears in this region, so carry a bell.

There's no wonder this is one of the most popular hiking trails of the Iseji route, or that it's UNESCO World Heritage-designated. The moss-covered Edo-period (1603–1868) flagstone path, lined with luscious ferns and cypress forest, ticks the boxes for a historic and scenic hike with superb views. It is possible to take a bus from the station to the trailhead, saving 2.3km, although figuring out the bus timetable may prove tricky.

Leave **Aiga station**, passing a payphone (RHS), and go straight (west). After 200m pass **Miyama Aiga** post office/

AIGA 相賀

Accommodation: Ryori Minshuku Sasaki 料理民宿ささき (tel 0597-32-1681, https://sasaki-sg.crayonsite.com/p/3/?, nine rooms, ¥¥ incl D&B, a 10min walk from Aiga station (pick-up available but no English spoken). Overlooking Lake Shiraishi, this delightful *minshuku* has a special emphasis on local fresh food).

ATM 海山相賀郵便局 (RHS). Shortly after, reach a junction with a row of VMs in front of Minzen liquor store みんぜん コンビマート (RHS) and turn left, passing a tall wooden Iseji marker on the RH corner of the shrine grounds (70km to Shingu 新宮まで/96km to Ise 伊勢まで). Pass **Aiga-jinja Shrine** 相賀神社 (RHS) and follow the road as it winds around for 300m to reach a T-junction

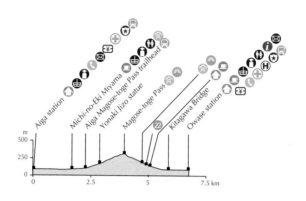

Café, supermarket, VM, WC, open daily 9am–7pm, the last place to buy any food/drinks.

Called 'night-crying Jizo', this was originally placed here to protect pilgrims and is now worshipped as a Jizo that can stop children from crying at night.

opposite the Choshi-gawa River 銚子川. Turn right, then left at the lights and cross the **Choshi bridge** 銚子橋, now on Route 42. Continue past a **Mazda dealership** マツダオートザム尾鷲 (LHS) and after a further 600m reach **Michi-no-Eki Miyama** road station 道の駅海山. ◀ **1.7km**

Continue along Route 42 for 600m to the **Magose-toge Pass trailhead** 馬越峠登り口 with a bilingual information board, stone marker (LHS) and **Washige** bus stop 鷲毛 バス停. Begin ascending the stone steps onto a stunning 2km stretch of *ishitatami* flagstone (see glossary), and after about 100m pass **Magose waymark 1** (RHS). Just after Magose waymark 4 (LHS), pass the **Yonaki Jizo statue** 夜泣き地蔵. ◀ **2.9km**

Cross the stone slab bridge over the stream and continue ascending, steeply at times. Between **Magose waymark 7** and 8, although hard to spot other than the Japanese sign, pass the **remains of an ichirizuka milestone mound** 馬越峠一里塚 where there was once a pine tree on the west side and a cherry tree on the east (see glossary). A few minutes later, go straight across a **forestry road** (with mountain views and benches), continuing up the stone path which alternates with a forest path

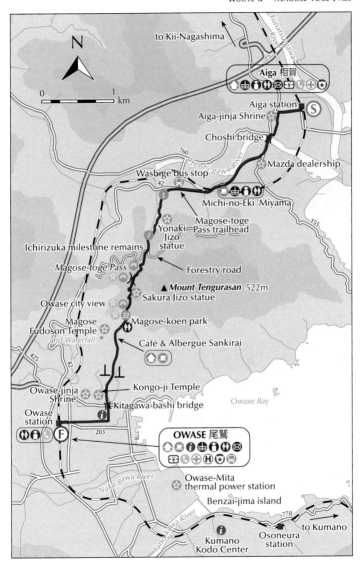

A rest shelter, teahouse remains and stamp box at Magose-toge Pass, where there are also terrific views of Owase city

on the way to Magose waymark 13 at **Magose-toge Pass** 馬越峠 (alt 325m) (rest shelter). **3.9km**

At **Magose-toge Pass** there are views of Owase and Mt Yakiyama (considered the hardest mountain of the Iseji), remains of a teahouse (which was popular with pilgrims until the middle of the Meiji period and sold *mochi* rice cakes) and a haiku poem monument (夜は花の上に音あり山の水, 'flowers of the night, sounds above, mountain water') written by Karyoen Toeitsu and engraved by his apprentice in the late Edo period while viewing the cherry blossom at night during their pilgrimage. There are also side-trails here to Mt Tengurasan 天狗倉山 (east, 30min each way, alt 522m) and Mt Binshiyama 便石山 (west, 2hr each way, alt 599m).

To descend to Owase, continue straight and down the stone path past a Japanese wooden sign reading '桜地蔵 550m 約 20 分' – 550m and 20min to Sakura Jizo. The path levels out with some benches at Magose waymark 15 if you need to give your knees a break; otherwise

continue down for a further 300m to reach Magose way-mark 18 and the **Sakura Jizo statue** 桜地蔵 (the statue is within a small brick house just across the stream). **4.4km**

Depending on recent rainfall, you may soon need to cross a stream on stepping stones. Shortly after passing Magose waymark 19 (LHS) there's a 40m detour (RHS) to a rest shelter and **viewpoint** 展望東屋 for a view of Owase city – not to be missed! On the main trail, continue descending to the last **Magose waymark (22)** with a rest shelter just up to the right. You're now in **Magose-koen park** 馬越公園 (WC). **4.8km**

Pass a white temple building (RHS) with a side-trail leading to the right through the *torii* gate to **Magose Fudoson Temple and Fudo no Taki Waterfall** 馬越峠 不動滝 (+100m). ▶ Retrace your steps to the main trail, then join a road and pass a WC and car park (LHS) with another tall wooden Iseji marker (LHS, 66km to Shingu 新宮まで/100km to Ise 伊勢まで). Continue down the steep road, following wooden signs towards 'Kita-gawa bashi bridge 熊野古道北川橋' and shortly after, pass a sign and side-trail (LHS) through the forest leading to Café/Albergue Sankirai 山帰来 (café open Fri–Sun

Owase city views from a rest shelter between Magose waymarks 19 and 20

Enshrined here is the seventh-century founder of Shugendo, En no Gyoja, as well as a statue of Fudo Myoo, one of the main Shugendo Buddhist deities.

205

10am–4pm). Go straight across the next road, then after a further 300m pass through a large **cemetery**. Continue following this road, through a short underpass, to reach a T-junction with the **Kitagawa-bashi bridge** 北川橋 (slightly left). ◀ **5.9km**

If you turn right here you'll reach Kongo-ji Temple 金剛寺 in 150m, then next door is Owase-jinja Shrine 尾鷲神社 – see 'Visit' below for details.

Cross the bridge into the built-up area of Owase and after 200m reach a tall wooden marker (RHS, pointing right for Owase station 尾鷲駅 680m/15min) on the corner of the **Owase Tourism and Product Association** 尾鷲観光物産協会 (with an orange sign). Turn right, following the wooden marker towards Owase station, along this narrow road into a shopping street 尾鷲南店街, passing local food stores. After 500m reach the end of the narrow road, merge straight onto a larger road and continue for 100m to reach **Owase** station 尾鷲駅 (VM, WC, payphone). **6.7km**

OWASE 尾鷲, 5M, POP 18,281

Known for its excessive annual rainfall (around 3850mm) and fresh seafood, Owase is a small city with a 'large town' feel and a few sights to warrant an afternoon or overnight stay after walking the Magose-toge Pass trail.

Tourist office: (Owase Tourism and Product Association) 尾鷲観光物産協会. On the Iseji trail in the middle of the city. The staff have a list of accommodation and maps, open daily 8.30am–5.15pm, tel 0597-23-8261.

Visit: Owase-jinja Shrine 尾鷲神社 – thought to have existed since the eighth century (records were destroyed in the great earthquake and tsunamis of 1707 and 1854), there's a large camphor tree (approximately 1000 years old) at the entrance and a large *taiko* (Japanese drum) inside the shrine. The city's largest annual festival, called Ya Ya Matsuri (1–5 Feb), starts here. **Kongo-ji Temple** 金剛寺 – next to Owase-jinja Shrine, with two red Nio guardian statues in the gate, it has the oldest temple bell in Owase. **Owase Itadaki market** – produce market held the first Saturday of each month at the fish market, 8.30am–12.30pm. **Kumano Kodo Center** 熊野古道センター – built from local cypress and cedar, this large modern centre has exhibitions, displays, a theatre and a state-of-the-art audio guide; it's just not so conveniently located! Tel 0597-25-2666, **www.kumanokodocenter.com/101117.html**, open daily 9am–5pm. Access: a 13min walk from Osoneura train station 大曽根浦駅, a 45min walk from Owase station,

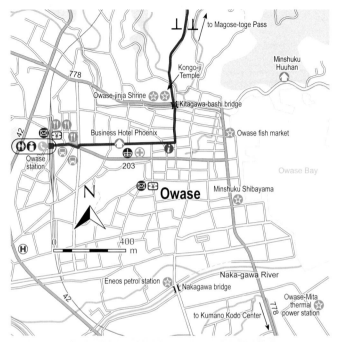

or 20min by bus from Owase station (two options): take the Fureai Bus ふれあいバス in front of Owase station (Owase-eki bus stop 尾鷲駅 バス停) bound for Kii-Matsumoto 紀伊松本; or take the Mie Kotsu Nanki Expressway Bus 南紀特急バス from Owase-eki-guchi bus stop 尾鷲駅口 バス停 bound for Kumano Kodo Center, 8min. With either bus, get off at Kumano Kodo Center-mae bus stop 熊野古道センター前 バス停.

Where to eat: the streets around the station are full of places to eat and drink, including Yoro-no-taki 養老乃瀧, an *izakaya* (pub) with a picture menu, opposite the small park, **www.yoronotaki.co.jp** (Japanese site).

Owase-jinja Shrine, Owase

Yakitori Daikichi やきとり大吉 (for chicken skewers), just around the corner from Yoro-no-taki, with a red-and-black sign, **www.daikichi.co.jp** (Japanese site). And next to Yakitori Daikichi is Oni Gawara 鬼瓦, for local seafood in a traditional setting. Yume Kodo Owase 夢古道おわせ is a popular café (and hot spring using sea water) behind the Kumano Kodo Center, open daily 9am–5pm (lunch buffet 11am–2pm), **http://yumekodo.jp/en**. There's also a Family Mart on Route 203, close to the station.

Accommodation: Albergue Sankirai アルベルゲ山帰来 (tel 0597-22-3597, **www. woodpeck.jp/albergue.htm** (Japanese site), two rooms, ¥ room only, located in a beautiful wooden cottage next to the café in the woods after descending from Magose-toge Pass). Minshuku Huuhan 民宿風帆 (tel 0597-22-2663, **www. huuhan.sakura.ne.jp** (Japanese site), 10 rooms, ¥¥ incl D&B, this renovated guesthouse overlooks the harbour and is a 9min walk from Kitagawa-bashi Bridge, near the Magose-toge Pass trailhead). Minshuku Shibayama 民宿柴山 (tel 0597-22-5566, seven rooms, ¥¥ incl D&B, attached to a fishing tour operator on the harbour, meals often include the daily catch). Business Hotel Phoenix ビジネスホテル フェニックス (tel 0597-22-8111, **www.bh-phoenix.com** (Japanese site), 31 rooms, ¥¥ room only, located behind the Family Mart (Route 203) close to Owase station).

ROUTE 6
Matsumoto-toge Pass 松本峠

Start	Odomari station 大泊駅
Finish	Arii station 有井駅
Distance	4.9km
Ascent	125m
Descent	130m
Difficulty	Easy
Duration	2–3hr
Access	Odomari 大泊駅 (+0.7km) is on the JR Kisei main line (one stop/3min from Kumanoshi 熊野市, or 40min from both Shingu 新宮 and Owase 尾鷲). Check the train schedule from Arii station in advance.
Waymarks	Between the station and the trailhead there are various bilingual waymarks, then there are wooden bilingual 'Matsumoto 松本峠' waymarks placed at 100m intervals counting from 1 to 7 over the pass. Waymarks are sporadic between Kumano and Arii.

This short but scenic walk on a flagstone path through a cedar forest sprinkled with bamboo is an easy way to get a taste of the Iseji trail, and there are fantastic sea views a few minutes from the top. There's an option to return along the cliffside Onigajo (demon's castle) walking trail. The stage also passes the Shishi-iwa lion rock as well as the ancient Hana-no-Iwaya-jinja Shrine, believed to be the grave of Izanami-no-Mikoto, the goddess that created Japan.

Leave **Odomari** station (payphone) and go straight down the road, passing a colourful information map (RHS). Pass a **Jizo statue** (LHS) then reach Route 311 with an Iseji stone marker 'Matsumoto-toge Pass 0.5km' and turn right. Pass VMs, go across the **Odomari-bashi bridge** 大泊橋, pass the **police station** 警察署 (RHS) and continue around to the left and uphill to the traffic lights. Use the

ODOMARI 大泊, 5M, POP 201

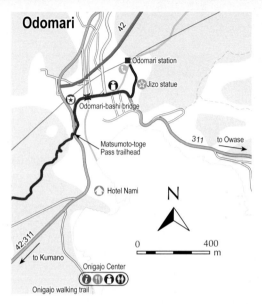

Accommodation: Hotel Nami ホテルなみ (tel 0597-88-1800, **www.hotel-nami. com** (Japanese site), 63 Western-style rooms with en-suite bathrooms, ¥¥¥ incl D&B. Located on a cliff a few minutes' walk from the trailhead in Odomari, this business/resort-style hotel includes a restaurant, coin laundry, VMs and ocean views).

pedestrian crossing here to reach the **Matsumoto-toge Pass trailhead** 松本峠登り口, where there's a Kumano Kodo Iseji marker indicating '26km to Shingu 新宮まで/ 140km to Ise 伊勢まで'. **700m**

Begin climbing the stone steps with a bamboo grove on the LHS, soon passing Matsumoto waymark 1 (RHS). Although it's not quite 500m to the pass, the steps are uneven and can be slippery; take your time and enjoy the Edo-period flagstone path. Shortly after Matsumoto waymark 4, reach **Matsumoto-toge Pass** 松本峠 (alt 135m). **1.2km**

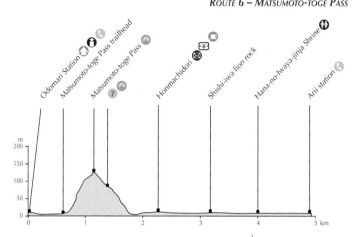

Odomari Station
Matsumoto-toge Pass trailhead
Matsumoto-toge Pass
Honmachidori
Shishi-iwa lion rock
Hana-no-Iwaya-jinja Shrine
Arii station

At **Matsumoto-toge Pass** there are teahouse remains, benches, a life-size Jizo statue, and a side-trail leading to a wonderful viewpoint of Kumano and the coast. The viewpoint is only a 4min walk

A hiker climbing the stone steps to Matsumoto-toge Pass

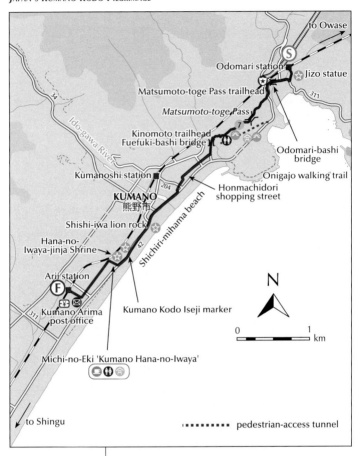

along the side-trail and is well worth it; follow the sign towards 'Onigajo castle ruins 鬼ケ城跡 700m'. (There's not much to see at the ruins.) Note that the Jizo at the pass has a hole near the base. According to legend, a hunter mistook the statue for a ghost in the mist and fired his gun!

To descend to Kumano, go down the stone steps following wooden signs to 'Kinomoto trailhead 木本登り口'. The moss-covered flagstone path soon resumes. Before long, reach **Matsumoto waymark 7/7** (RHS) with a viewpoint opposite, then join a road and pass a WC (LHS). Continue as the road becomes a winding stone path, reaching the bottom on a small road between houses at the **Kinomoto trailhead** 木本登り口. Go straight and across the small concrete **Fuefuki-bashi bridge** 笛吹橋. **1.8km**

According to **legend**, during the Heian period the site where Onigajo castle was later built was the lair of a demon that tormented villagers. An army was sent to deal with the problem without success – the caves provided endless hiding places and the tempestuous sea made an attack by boat impossible. One day, a beautiful Buddhist guardian appeared in the sky, drawing out the curious demon which was shot with an arrow. The army celebrated by playing flutes and drums on Fuefuki-bashi bridge, so it came to be known as 'whistle-blowing bridge' (the round holes in the railings represent flutes).

Follow the road, passing houses as you enter an old neighbourhood of Kumano City, and before reaching the end, turn right opposite Hamanaka はまなか noodle restaurant (LHS) onto the **Honmachidori** 本町通り shopping street.

Take the first right for the **Kinan Tour Design Center** 紀南ツアーデザインセンター, a local-area information centre in a traditional 19th-century house, open daily except Wednesdays 9am–5pm, www.kinan-tdc.com (Japanese site).

KUMANO 熊野, 9M, POP 17,367

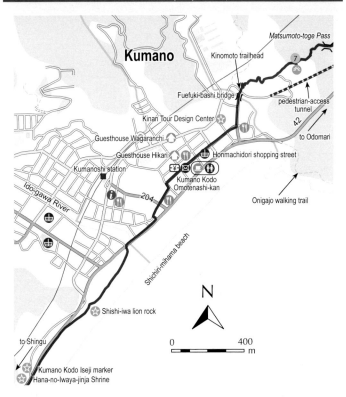

Kumano feels more like an old, quiet town than a city but has ample facilities and terrific World Heritage natural sites on its doorstep. If you cross Matsumoto-toge Pass in the morning, you'll have plenty of time to see the other sites in the afternoon.

Tourist office: Kumano City Tourist Association 熊野市観光協会, opposite Kumanoshi train station 熊野市駅, has English-speaking staff, maps and bicycle rental, tel 0597-89-0100, **www.kumano-kankou-enzh.jimdo.com**, open daily 9am–5pm.

The Onigajo walking trail, Kumano (photo: Howard Miller)

Visit: Onigajo walking trail 鬼ヶ城遊歩道 where it is easy to see how people believed the cave formations were inhabited by *oni* (demons). The 1.2km/45min trail starts from the **Onigajo Center** 鬼ヶ城センタ further up the coastal road from Hotel Nami on the Odomari side (café, restaurant and tourist information, open daily 9am–5pm, tel 0597-89-1502, **www.onigajyo.mie.jp** (Japanese site)) and ends on the Kumano side, but you can walk either direction.

Where to eat: Kiraku 喜楽, next to the tourist office opposite Kumanoshi station, serves a variety of meals including local sushi specialities. Hana-no-Iwaya Tei 花のいわや亭, on Route 42 just past Hana-no-Iwaya Shrine, is a large restaurant with an extensive menu including Kumano Sanzan set meals, open daily 11am– 2pm & 5–11pm, **www.hananoiwayatei.com** (Japanese site). Mos Burger モスバーガー, on Route 42 (6min from Kumanoshi station), is a Japanese burger chain that serves, in addition to regular burgers, local variants using rice paddies for the bun!

Accommodation: (the following two guesthouses don't have bathrooms but there are public bathhouses nearby): Guesthouse Wagaranchi わがらん家 (tel 090-1471-4889, four rooms, ¥ room only, located a 7min walk from Kumanoshi station). Guesthouse Hikari 熊野ひかり (tel 0597-89-5515, eight rooms, ¥ room only, there is a Japanese restaurant onsite). **Resort Kumano Club** 里創人 熊野倶楽部 (tel 0597-88-2045, **www.resortkumanoclub.com**, 40 rooms, ¥¥¥¥ incl D&B, a luxurious resort with a restaurant, *onsen*, bike hire, tours of the nearby Kumano Kodo trails and free shuttle service to/from Kumanoshi station).

For Kumanoshi station 熊野市駅 or Kumano City tourist office 熊野市観光協会 (opposite the station), take the next right and continue for 320m to the end of the street.

Continue along Honmachidori, and after 300m, just before Kumano Honmachi post office/ATM 熊野本町郵便局 (LHS), pass **Kumano Kodo Omotenashi-kan** 熊野古道 おもてなし館 (LHS). Inside this traditional house is a rest area, information, local products and a café, open daily except Mondays, 9.30am–4.30pm. **2.3km**

Turn left at the end of the road then take the first right. ◄ Take the second left and reach Route 42 and the sea wall.

Shichiri-mihama beach is behind the sea wall. Meaning 'seven *ri* beach', a *ri* is an old measurement of distance: one *ri* is approximately 3.9km, so 7 *ri* is around 27km – although the pebble beach is actually 22km long.

Shishi-iwa lion rock

Turn right and either walk along the sea wall or footpath, passing restaurants. After 600m pass the famous **Shishi-iwa lion rock** 獅子岩. ▸ **3.3km**

Continue along Route 42, following green markers on the pavement to Hana-no-Iwaya, and after 600m pass a **Kumano Kodo Iseji marker** (RHS, '22km to Shingu 新宮まで/144km to Ise 伊勢まで'). Turn right at the next traffic lights and pass **Michi-no-Eki Kumano Hana-no-Iwaya rest station** 道の駅 熊野 花の窟 (also called Otsunachaya お綱茶屋, café open daily 10am–5pm) located opposite **Hana-no-Iwaya-jinja Shrine** 花の窟神社. **4km**

> Considered the oldest shrine in Japan, written references to **Hana-no-Iwaya-jinja Shrine** date back to one of Japan's oldest books, the eighth-century *Nihon Shoki*. The name means 'cave of flowers', and the site is believed to be the grave of Izanami-no-Mikoto, the goddess that gave birth to the islands of Japan. The 45m-tall boulder has been worshipped since ancient times. The *shimenawa* (sacred Shinto rope) tied across the top features in two annual festivals (2 February and 2 October, also mentioned in the *Nihon Shoki*), during which it is pulled across to the beach – you can see this depicted on the *ema* votive tablets.

Depending on the infrequent trains and where you are staying, you may wish to backtrack to more facilities in Kumano City and the busier station of Kumanoshi; or for Arii station, continue along this road as it bends left, then after a further 500m go straight across the small junction with traffic lights. Take the next right (if you pass Kumano Arima post office 熊野有馬郵便局, you've gone too far) and after 180m reach the end of the road at **Arii station** 有井駅. (This is a tiny station with just a payphone.) **4.9km**

The 25m-high Shishi-iwa lion rock resembles a lion roaring and gazing over the sea.

APPENDIX A

Facilities tables

Nakahechi

Place	Distance from last place (km)	Accommodatio
Tanabe 田辺	*by bus*	x
Takijiri-oji 滝尻王子	*by bus*	x
Takahara 高原	3.7	x
Michi-no-Eki 'Kumano Kodo Nakahechi' road station (Route 311) 道の駅熊野古道中辺路	7.7	
Chikatsuyu 近露	1.5	x
Tsugizakura-oji/Nonaka 継桜王子/野中	3.4	x
Hosshinmon-oji 発心門王子	13.6	
Hongu 本宮	6.8	x
Yunomine Onsen 湯の峰温泉	2.8 (Dainichi-goe route)	x
Wataze Onsen 渡瀬温泉	2.2	x
Kawayu Onsen 川湯温泉	1	x
Ukegawa 請川	2.3	x
Kowase 小和	11.7	
Koguchi 小口	0.9	x
Jizo-jaya teahouse remains 地蔵茶屋跡	6.2	
Nachisan 那智山	8	x

Nearby areas

Nachi station 那智駅	*by bus/train*	
Nachi-Katsuura 那智勝浦	*by bus/train*	x
Shingu 新宮	*by bus/train*	x

Choishimichi

Place	Distance from last place (km)	Accommodatio
Kudoyama station 九度山駅	0	
Michi-no-Eki Kaki-no-Sato Kudoyama road station 道の駅柿の郷九度山	1	
Yatate 矢立	13.5	
Koyasan 高野山	5.7	x

Vending machine	Café or restaurant	Supermarket or local shop	Post office (ATM)	Pharmacy or drugstore	Tourist office	Payphone
X	X	X	X	X	X	X
X		X			X	
X	X					X
X	X	X				X
X	X	X	X			X
X						
X	X	X	X	X	X	X
X	X	X				X
X	X					X
X	X					X
X	X	X	X			X
X						
X		X	X			X
X						
X	X		X			X
X	X	X			X	X
X	X	X	X	X	X	X
X	X	X	X	X	X	X

Vending machine	Café or restaurant	Supermarket or local shop	Post office (ATM)	Pharmacy or drugstore	Tourist office	Payphone
X						
X	X	X				X
X	X					
X	X	X	X	X	X	X

Kohechi

Place	Distance from last place (km)	Distance from Koyasan	Accommodation	Vending machine
Koyasan 高野山	0	0	x	x
Omata 大股	16.8	16.8	x	x
Miura-guchi 三浦口	14	30.8	x	x
Nishinaka 西中	10.3	41.1		x
Nagai 永井	1.8	42.9		x
Shigesato 重里	1.3	44.2		x
Subaru no Sato 昴の郷	4.5	48.7	x	x
Totsukawa Onsen (off-trail) 十津川温泉	2	50.7	x	x
Michi-no-Eki 'Oku Kumano Kodo Hongu' road station 道の駅奥熊野古道ほんぐう	11.1	59.8		x
Hongu 本宮	3.6	63.4	x	x

Iseji – Magose-toge Pass

Place	Distance from last place (km)	Accommodation	Vending machine
Aiga 相賀	0	x	x
Michi-no-Eki Miyama road station 道の駅海山	1.7		x
Owase 尾鷲	5	x	x

Iseji – Matsumoto-toge Pass

Place	Distance from last place (km)	Accommodation	Vending machine
Odomari station 大泊駅	0	x	x
Kumano City 熊野	2	x	x
Arii 有井	2.9		

Café or restaurant	Supermarket or local shop	Post office (ATM)	Pharmacy or drugstore	Tourist office	Payphone	Distance to Hongu
x	x	x	x	x	x	63.4
					x	46.6
	x				x	32.6
	x				x	22.3
	x					20.5
		x			x	19.2
x	x				x	14.7
x	x	x	x		x	16.7
x	x				x	3.6
x	x	x	x	x	x	0

Café or restaurant	Supermarket or local shop	Post office (ATM)	Pharmacy or drugstore	Tourist office	Payphone
	x	x	x		x
x	x				x
x	x	x	x	x	x

Café or restaurant	Supermarket or local shop	Post office (ATM)	Pharmacy or drugstore	Tourist office	Payphone
					x
x	x	x	x	x	x
		x			x

APPENDIX B
Glossary

The pilgrimage trails

pronounced	Japanese	English
ari-no-Kumano mode	蟻の熊野詣	'procession of ants to Kumano', referring to the popularity of the pilgrimage
chaya	茶屋	teahouses that were established to provide pilgrims with food (mochi rice cakes, manju steamed buns, fruit and anything grown locally), tea, alcohol and replacement waraji straw sandals, as well as a place to rest – the equivalent of today's roadside stations or cafés
cho	丁	an old measurement of distance; one cho is about 109m
choishi	丁石/ 町石	a milestone that uses the old cho measurement of distance
haiku	俳句	Japanese poetry made up of 5–7–5 syllables
hashi/bashi	橋	bridge
hatago	旅籠	inns that provided accommodation and meals for commoners during the Edo period
ichirizuka milestone	一里塚跡	mounds of dirt on each side of a road, often with trees planted to provide shade and typically spaced at a distance of one ri (about 3.9km)
ishigaki	石垣	stone walls (see shishigaki)
ishitatami flagstone	石畳	many of the surviving flagstone paths were laid in the Edo period when the Kishu Clan, under the leadership of Tokugawa Yorinobu (1602–1671), set out to redevelop the Kumano Kodo roads, marking a resurgence in pilgrims: flagstone was laid to protect the paths from erosion in these heavy rainfall areas
kawa/gawa	川	river
Kumano Bikuni	熊野比丘尼	the name given to the travelling nuns who used mandalas (iconography) to spread the Kumano faith throughout Japan from the 16th to 18th centuries

pronounced	Japanese	English
Kumano Kodo	熊野古道	old roads to Kumano
Kumano Mode	熊野詣	Kumano pilgrimage
Kumano Sankeimichi	熊野参詣道	Kumano pilgrimage roads
Kumano Sanzan	熊野三山	the three grand shrines of Kumano: Kumano Hongu Taisha, Kumano Hayatama Taisha and Kumano Nachi Taisha
ri	里	an old measurement of distance; one ri is about 3.9km (36 cho) – see cho and ichiri-zuka for more details
Saigoku Junrei	西国巡礼	33 Kannon Pilgrimage of Western Japan – Japan's oldest pilgrimage, believed to have begun in the year 718 by Saint Tokudo Shonin (it celebrated 1300 years in 2018): the pilgrimage covers around 1000km and visits the 33 manifestations of Kannon, the Bodhisattva of mercy and compassion. Seiganto-ji Temple next to Nachi Taisha is number one of the 33 temples.
sekisho	関所	checkpoints to collect tolls were established along the Kumano Kodo as early as the 15th century: during the late Edo period, the toll was 10 mon which equates to ¥200 today. There are checkpoint remnants along the Nakahechi at Mikoshi-toge, Sangenjaya and along the Daimonzaka path.
shishigaki	猪垣	constructed in rural areas to keep wild boars away from crops
taisha	大社	grand shrine
tenmasho	伝馬所	horse post station: along the Nakahechi route between Tanabe and Hongu there were a number of tenmasho established during the Edo period: horses were used to travel from one station to the next, delivering official documents, packages, or people
Yamabushi	山伏	'mountain priest' – a person who practises Shugendo

Useful words and phrases

English	pronounced	Japanese
good morning	ohayou gozaimasu	おはようございます
good afternoon/hello	konnichiwa	こんにちは
good evening	konbanwa	こんばんは
good night	oyasuminasai	おやすみなさい
goodbye	sayounara	さようなら
please	kudasai/onegaishimasu	ください/お願いします
thank you	arigatou gozaimasu	ありがとうございます
you're welcome	dou-itashi-mashite	どういたしまして
how are you?	ogenki desu ka?	お元気ですか?
I'm good	genki desu	元気です
excuse me/sorry	sumimasen	すみません
I'm sorry	gomen-nasai	ごめんなさい
yes	hai	はい
no	iie	いいえ
my name is...	watashi no namae wa... desu	私の名前は…
nice to meet you	hajime-mashite	はじめまして
where is the...?	... wa doko desu ka?	… はどこですか?

English	pronounced	Japanese
there has been an accident	jiko ga arimashita	事故がありました
I'm injured	kega o shimashita	ケガをしました
please call an ambulance	kyuukyuusha o yonde kudasai	救急車を呼んでください
toilet	toire/o te arai	トイレ/お手洗い
post office	yubinkyoku	郵便局
pharmacy	kusuriya/yakkyoku	薬屋/薬局
supermarket/convenience store	supaamaketto/konbini	スーパーマーケット/コンビニ
bus stop	basu tei	バス停
I don't understand Japanese	watashi wa nihongo ga wakarimasen	私は日本語がわかりません
do you speak English?	eigo ga hanasemasu ka?	英語が話せますか?
please say it again	mou ichido itte kudasai	もう一度言ってください
please speak slowly	yukkuri itte kudasai	ゆっくり言ってください
I understand	wakarimasu	わかります
I don't understand	wakarimasen	わかりません
please wait a moment	chotto matte kudasai	ちょっと待ってください
how much does this cost?	kore wa ikura desu ka?	これはいくらですか?

Food and drinks

English	pronounced	Japanese
bon appetit	itadakimasu	いただきます
thank you for the meal	gochisousamadeshita	ごちそうさまでした
delicious	oishii	おいしい
bill please	o kanjou kudasai	お勘定下さい
Japanese-style food	washoku	和食
Western-style food	youshoku	洋食
breakfast	asa-gohan	朝ごはん
lunch	ranchi/hirugohan	ランチ/昼ごはん
dinner	di-naa/yushoku	ディナー/夕食
rice	raisu/gohan	ライス/ご飯
miso soup	miso-shiru	みそ汁
fish	sakana	魚
fish – grilled	yaki-sakana	焼き魚
fish – raw	nama-no-sakana	生の魚
eggs	tamago	卵
eggs – boiled	ude tamago	ゆで卵
eggs – raw	nama tamago	生卵
eggs – scrambled	sukuranburu eggu	スクランブルエッグ
eggs – fried	medama-yaki	目玉焼き
pickles	tsukemono	漬物
mountain vegetables	sansai	山菜
rice balls with fillings	onigiri	おにぎり
sandwich	sandoitchi	サンドイッチ
ham	hamu	ハム
cheese	chiizu	チーズ
water	mizu	水
coffee	kouhi	コーヒー

English	pronounced	Japanese
tea	ocha	お茶
orange juice	orenji juusu	オレンジジュース
coke	kora	コーラ
beer	beeru	ビール
Japanese rice wine	sake	日本酒

Numbers

English	pronounced	Japanese
one	ichi	一
two	ni	二
three	san	三
four	shi/yon	四
five	go	五
six	roku	六
seven	nana/shichi	七
eight	hachi	八
nine	kyu	九
ten	juu	十
twenty	ni-juu	二十
thirty	san-juu	三十
forty	yon-juu	四十
fifty	go-juu	五十
sixty	roku-juu	六十
seventy	nana-juu	七十
eighty	hachi-juu	八十
ninety	kyū-juu	九十
one hundred	hyaku	百
one thousand	sen	千
ten thousand	ichi man	1万

APPENDIX C
Useful contacts

Kumano Kodo information and maps
www.tb-kumano.jp/en

Dual Pilgrim Spiritual Pilgrimages website
http://dual-pilgrim.spiritual-pilgrimages.com

Transport

Air
Kansai International Airport, Osaka
www.kansai-airport.or.jp/en

Narita International Airport, near Tokyo
www.narita-airport.jp/en

Haneda Airport, Tokyo
www.haneda-airport.jp/en

Nanki Shirahama airport, Shirahama
www.shirahama-airport.jp

All Nippon Airways (ANA)
www.ana.co.jp/en/gb

Japan Airlines
www.jal.co.jp/en

British Airways
www.britishairways.com

Jetstar (Australia)
www.jetstar.com

Bus
Kansai Airport Transportation Enterprise
www.kate.co.jp/en

Koyasan to Hongu
https://japanbusonline.com/en

Willer Express
www.willerexpress.com

Rail
West Japan Rail
www.westjr.co.jp/global/en

Hyperdia – train timetables in English
www.hyperdia.com

Weather
Japan Meteorological Agency (JMA)
www.jma.go.jp/jma/indexe.html

Japan National Tourism Organization (JNTO)
www.jnto.go.jp/weather/eng/index.php
(see 'Kansai Area'; 'Wakayama')

Luggage transfer
Kumano Travel
www.kumano-travel.com/en

Takkyubin 宅急便
www.global-yamato.com

Guided tours

Nakahechi
Oku Japan
www.okujapan.com

Walks Worldwide
www.walksworldwide.com

Walk Japan
https://walkjapan.com

National Geographic Expeditions
www.nationalgeographicexpeditions.com

Kohechi
Great Hikes Japan
www.greathikesjapan.com

Oku Japan
www.okujapan.com

Koyasan
Day and night tours led by Buddhist monks
https://awesome-tours.jp/en

Daytime and hiking tours
www.koyasan-ccn.com/guided-tours

Self-guided tours

Nakahechi
Inside Japan
www.insidejapantours.com

Oku Japan
www.okujapan.com

Macs Adventure
www.macsadventure.com

Raw Travel
www.rawtravel.com

Samurai Tours
www.samuraitours.com

Local guides
Kumano Experience
(hiking, sea/river kayaking and custom tours)
www.kumano-experience.com/WP2017/en

Mi-Kumano
(1/2 to 5 days hiking guides)
https://en.mi-kumano.com

Wakayama and Koyasan Guide
www.wak-guide.com

Tourist offices (dialling code +81)

Nakahechi route
Tanabe
Tanabe Tourist Information Center
田辺市熊野ツーリズムビューロー
next to Kii-Tanabe station
tel 0739-26-9025
www.tb-kumano.jp/en
Mon–Fri 9am–5pm

Kurisugawa
Kumano Kodo Kan Pilgrimage Center
熊野古道館
opposite Takijiri-oji
tel 0739-64-1470
daily 8.30am–5pm

Hongu
Kumano Hongu Heritage Center 世界遺産 熊野本宮館
opposite Kumano Hongu Taisha
tel 0735-42-0751
www.city.tanabe.lg.jp/hongukan/en
daily 8.30am–5pm

Shingu
Shingu City Tourist Information Center
熊野新宮観光案内センター
opposite Shingu station
tel 0735-22-2840
www.shinguu.jp/en
daily 9am–5pm

Nachi-Katsuura
Nachi-Katsuura Tourist Information Center
那智勝浦町観光協会
on the ground floor of Kii-Katsuura station
tel 0735-52-5311
www.nachikan.jp/en
daily 8.30am–6pm

Koyasan

Koyasan Shukubo Association
高野山宿坊協会
Three locations: the central office is in the main street by Senjuinbashi bus stop and the other two locations are opposite Ichinohashi and Nakanohashi entrances to Okunoin
tel 0736-56-2616
http://eng.shukubo.net
daily 8.30am–5pm (Mar–Nov) or 9am–5pm (Dec–Feb)

Koyasan Visitor Information Center
高野山ビジターインフォメーションセンター
on the first floor of the Daishi Kyokai Center
tel 0736-56-2270
www.koyasan-ccn.com
daily (except Tues & Thurs) 10am–4pm (Apr–Nov) or Wed & Fri 10am–4pm (Dec–Mar)

Iseji route

Magose-toge Pass
Owase
Owase Tourism and Product Association
尾鷲観光物産協会
tel 0597-23-8261
open daily 8.30am–5.15pm

Owase
Kumano Kodo Center
熊野古道センター
Closest station: Osoneura
tel 0597-25-2666
www.kumanokodocenter.com/101117.html
daily 9am–5pm

Matsumoto-toge Pass
Kumano City
Kumano City Tourist Association
熊野市観光協会
opposite Kumanoshi train station
tel 0597-89-0100
www.kumano-kankou-enzh.jimdo.com
daily 9am–5pm

Post offices with ATMs

See www.post.japanpost.jp/index_en.html

Nakahechi route

Tanabe (closest to the station)
Tanabe eki mae yubinkyoku
田辺駅前郵便局
Mon–Fri 9am–5pm
ATM: Mon–Fri 9am–5.30pm, Sat 9am–12.30pm

Tanabe (10min walk from the station)
Tanabe yubinkyoku
田辺郵便局
Mon–Fri 9am–7pm, Sat 9am–3pm
ATM: Mon–Fri 8am–9pm, Sat–Sun 9am–7pm

Chikatsuyu
Chikatsuyu yubinkyoku
近露郵便局
Mon–Fri 9am–5pm
ATM: Mon–Fri 9am–5.30pm, Sat 9am–12.30pm

Hongu
Hongu yubinkyoku
本宮郵便局
Mon–Fri 9am–5pm
ATM: Mon–Fri 8.45am–6pm, Sat 9am–5pm, Sun 9am–3pm

Ukegawa
Ukegawa yubinkyoku
請川郵便局
Mon–Fri 9am–5pm
ATM: Mon–Fri 9am–5.30pm,
Sat 9am–12.30pm

Koguchi
Koguchi yubinkyoku
小口郵便局
Mon–Fri 9am–5pm
ATM: Mon–Fri 9am–5.30pm,
Sat 9am–12.30pm

Nachisan
Nachisan yubinkyoku
那智山郵便局
Mon–Fri 9am–5pm
ATM: Mon–Fri 9am–5.30pm,
Sat 9am–12.30pm

Katsuura (closest to the station)
Kii-Katsuura yubinkyoku
紀伊勝浦郵便局
Mon–Fri 9am–5pm
ATM: Mon–Fri 8.45am–7pm, Sat–Sun
9am–5pm

Katsuura (near the port)
Nachi-Katsuura Minato yubinkyoku
那智勝浦港郵便局
Mon–Fri 9am–5pm
ATM: Mon–Fri 9am–5.30pm,
Sat 9am–12.30pm

Shingu (closest to the station)
Shingu yubinkyoku
新宮郵便局
Mon–Fri 9am–7pm
ATM: Mon–Fri 8.45am–7pm, Sat–Sun
9am–7pm

Shingu (closest to Hayatama Taisha)
Shingu Yokomachi yubinkyoku
新宮横町郵便局
Mon–Fri 9am–5pm
ATM: Mon–Fri 9am–5.30pm,
Sat 9am–12.30pm

Kohechi route

Koyasan
Koya yubinkyoku
高野郵便局
Mon–Fri 9am–5pm
ATM: Mon–Fri 8.45am–6pm,
Sat 9am–5pm, Sun 9am–3pm

Shigesato
Shigesato yubinkyoku
重里郵便局
Mon–Fri 9am–5pm
ATM: Mon–Fri 8.45am–6pm, Sat
9am–2pm

Totsukawa Onsen
Hiratani yubinkyoku
平谷郵便局
Mon–Fri 9am–5pm
ATM: Mon–Fri 8.45am–6pm, Sat
9am–2pm

Iseji route

Magose-toge Pass
Aiga
Miyama Aiga yubinkyoku
海山相賀郵便局
Mon–Fri 9am–5pm
ATM: Mon–Fri 9am–5.30pm,
Sat 9am–12.30pm

Owase (closest to Owase station)
Owase eki-mae yubinkyoku
尾鷲駅前郵便局
Mon–Fri 9am–5pm
ATM: Mon–Fri 9am–5.30pm,
Sat 9am–12.30pm

Owase (8min walk from the station)
Owase yubinkyoku
尾鷲郵便局
Mon–Fri 9am–7pm
ATM: Mon–Fri 8.45am–7pm, Sat,
Sun and holidays 9am–5pm

Matsumoto-toge Pass
Kumano
Kumano Honmachi yubinkyoku
熊野本町郵便局
Mon–Fri 9am–5pm
ATM: Mon–Fri 9am–5.30pm,
Sat 9am–12.30pm

Near Arii station
Kumano Arima yubinkyoku
熊野有馬郵便局
Mon–Fri 9am–5pm
ATM: Mon–Fri 9am–5.30pm, Sat
9am–12.30pm

Medical assistance
The following link allows you to search for hospitals and clinics with English-speaking staff by prefecture (the Nakahechi and Koyasan are in Wakayama Prefecture, the Kohechi is in Wakayama and Nara Prefectures, the Iseji is in Mie Prefecture): www. jnto.go.jp/emergency/eng/mi_guide. html#search

Japan Helpline operates a 24-hour nationwide English-language assistance service for the international community and can also help in an emergency situation: tel 0570-00-0911.

Emergencies
Fire (*kaji*)
119

Medical emergency (*kyukyu*)
119

Police (*keisatsu*)
110

APPENDIX D
Further reading

Tanabe City (Brad Towle), *Kumano Kodo Nakahechi: Official Guide Book* (TREE Inc, 2017)

General travel
Rebecca Milner et al, *Lonely Planet Japan* (Lonely Planet, 2017)

Jan Dodd, Martin Zatko et al, *The Rough Guide to Japan* (Rough Guides, 2017)

Ramsey Zarifen and Anna Udagawa, *Japan by Rail*, (Trailblazer Publications, 2016)

Spirituality
Helen Hardacre, *Shinto: A history* (Oxford University Press, 2017)

Thomas P Kasulis, *Shinto: The Way Home* (University of Hawaii Press, 2004)

Motohisa Yamakage, *The Essence of Shinto: Japan's Spiritual Heart* (Kodansha, 2012)

Kamata Toji, *Myth and Deity in Japan: The Interplay of Kami and Buddhas* (Japan Publishing Industry Foundation for Culture, 2017)

Elizabeth ten Grotenhuis, *Japanese Mandalas: Representations of Sacred Geography* (University of Hawaii Press, 1999)

Philip L Nicoloff, *Sacred Koyasan: A Pilgrimage to the Mountain Temple of Saint Kobo Daishi and the Great Sun Buddha* (State University of New York Press, 2008)

History
William E Deal, *Handbook to Life in Medieval and Early Modern Japan* (Oxford University Press, 2006)

Alex Kerr, *Lost Japan: Last Glimpse of Beautiful Japan* (Penguin, 2015)

Jonathan Clements, *A Brief History of Japan, Samurai, Shogun and Zen: The Extraordinary Story of the Land of the Rising Sun* (Tuttle Publishing, 2017)

Donald H. Shively (ed.) and William H. McCullough (ed.), *The Cambridge History of Japan, Volume 2: Heian Japan* (Cambridge University Press, 1999)

Kozo Yamamura (ed.), *The Cambridge History of Japan, Volume 3: Medieval Japan* (Cambridge University Press, 1990)

John Whitney Hall (ed.), *The Cambridge History of Japan, Volume 4: Early Modern Japan* (Cambridge University Press, 1991)

Culture
Engelbert Kaempfer – edited, translated and annotated by Beatrice M Bodart-Bailey, *Kaempfer's Japan: Tokugawa Culture Observed* (University of Hawaii Press, 1999)

William R Lafleur, *Awesome Nightfall: The Life, Times and Poetry of Saigyo* (Wisdom Publications, 2003)

DOWNLOAD THE ROUTES
IN GPX FORMAT

All the routes in this guide are available for download from:

www.cicerone.co.uk/972/GPX

as GPX files. You should be able to load them into most formats of mobile device, whether GPS or smartphone.

When you go to this link, you will be asked for your email address and where you purchased the guide, and have the option to subscribe to the Cicerone e-newsletter.

www.cicerone.co.uk

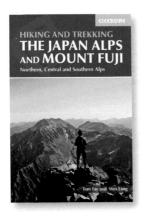
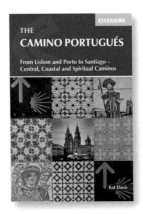

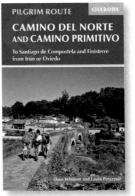

LISTING OF CICERONE GUIDES

SCOTLAND

Backpacker's Britain:
  Northern Scotland
Ben Nevis and Glen Coe
Cycling in the Hebrides
Great Mountain Days in Scotland
Mountain Biking in Southern and
  Central Scotland
Mountain Biking in West and
  North West Scotland
Not the West Highland Way
Scotland
Scotland's Best Small Mountains
Scotland's Mountain Ridges
Scrambles in Lochaber
The Ayrshire and Arran Coastal
  Paths
The Border Country
The Borders Abbeys Way
The Cape Wrath Trail
The Great Glen Way
The Great Glen Way Map Booklet
The Hebridean Way
The Hebrides
The Isle of Mull
The Isle of Skye
The Skye Trail
The Southern Upland Way
The Speyside Way
The Speyside Way Map Booklet
The West Highland Way
Walking Highland Perthshire
Walking in Scotland's Far North
Walking in the Angus Glens
Walking in the Cairngorms
Walking in the Ochils, Campsie
  Fells and Lomond Hills
Walking in the Pentland Hills
Walking in the Southern Uplands
Walking in Torridon
Walking Loch Lomond and the
  Trossachs
Walking on Arran
Walking on Harris and Lewis
Walking on Rum and the Small
  Isles
Walking on the Orkney and
  Shetland Isles
Walking on Uist and Barra
Walking the Corbetts Vol 1 South
  of the Great Glen
Walking the Corbetts Vol 2 North
  of the Great Glen
Walking the Munros
  Vol 1 – Southern, Central and
  Western Highlands
Walking the Munros
  Vol 2 – Northern Highlands
  and the Cairngorms

West Highland Way Map Booklet
Winter Climbs Ben Nevis and
  Glen Coe
Winter Climbs in the Cairngorms

NORTHERN ENGLAND TRAILS

Hadrian's Wall Path
Hadrian's Wall Path Map Booklet
Pennine Way Map Booklet
The Coast to Coast Map Booklet
The Coast to Coast Walk
The Dales Way
The Dales Way Map Booklet
The Pennine Way

LAKE DISTRICT

Cycling in the Lake District
Great Mountain Days in the Lake
  District
Lake District Winter Climbs
Lake District: High Level and
  Fell Walks
Lake District: Low Level and
  Lake Walks
Mountain Biking in the Lake
  District
Outdoor Adventures with
  Children – Lake District
Scrambles in the Lake District
  – North
Scrambles in the Lake District
  – South
Short Walks in Lakeland
  Book 1: South Lakeland
Short Walks in Lakeland
  Book 2: North Lakeland
Short Walks in Lakeland
  Book 3: West Lakeland
The Cumbria Way
Tour of the Lake District
Trail and Fell Running in the Lake
  District

NORTH WEST ENGLAND
AND THE ISLE OF MAN

Cycling the Pennine Bridleway
Cycling the Way of the Roses
Isle of Man Coastal Path
The Lancashire Cycleway
The Lune Valley and Howgills
The Ribble Way
Walking in Cumbria's Eden Valley
Walking in Lancashire
Walking in the Forest of Bowland
  and Pendle
Walking on the Isle of Man
Walking on the West Pennine
  Moors
Walks in Ribble Country
Walks in Silverdale and Arnside

NORTH EAST ENGLAND,
YORKSHIRE DALES
AND PENNINES

Cycling in the Yorkshire Dales
Great Mountain Days in the
  Pennines
Mountain Biking in the Yorkshire
  Dales
South Pennine Walks
St Oswald's Way and
  St Cuthbert's Way
The Cleveland Way and the
  Yorkshire Wolds Way
The Cleveland Way Map Booklet
The North York Moors
The Reivers Way
The Teesdale Way
Trail and Fell Running in the
  Yorkshire Dales
Walking in County Durham
Walking in Northumberland
Walking in the North Pennines
Walking in the Yorkshire Dales:
  North and East
Walking in the Yorkshire Dales:
  South and West
Walks in Dales Country
Walks in the Yorkshire Dales

WALES AND WELSH BORDERS

Cycling Lôn Las Cymru
Glyndwr's Way
Great Mountain Days in
  Snowdonia
Hillwalking in Shropshire
Hillwalking in Wales – Vol 1
Hillwalking in Wales – Vol 2
Mountain Walking in Snowdonia
Offa's Dyke Map Booklet
Offa's Dyke Path
Ridges of Snowdonia
Scrambles in Snowdonia
The Ascent of Snowdon
The Ceredigion and Snowdonia
  Coast Paths
The Pembrokeshire Coast Path
Pembrokeshire Coast Path Map
  Booklet
The Severn Way
The Snowdonia Way
The Wales Coast Path
The Wye Valley Walk
Walking in Carmarthenshire
Walking in Pembrokeshire
Walking in the Forest of Dean
Walking in the South Wales
  Valleys
Walking in the Wye Valley
Walking on the Brecon Beacons
Walking on the Gower

ICELAND AND GREENLAND

Trekking in Greenland –
   The Arctic Circle Trail
Walking and Trekking in Iceland

IRELAND

The Irish Coast to Coast Walk
The Mountains of Ireland
The Wild Atlantic Way and
   Western Ireland

ITALY

Italy's Sibillini National Park
Shorter Walks in the Dolomites
Ski Touring and Snowshoeing in
   the Dolomites
The Way of St Francis
Through the Italian Alps
Trekking in the Apennines
Trekking in the Dolomites
Via Ferratas of the Italian
   Dolomites: Vol 1
Via Ferratas of the Italian
   Dolomites: Vol 2
Walking and Trekking in the Gran
   Paradiso
Walking in Abruzzo
Walking in Italy's Stelvio National
   Park
Walking in Sardinia
Walking in Sicily
Walking in the Dolomites
Walking in Tuscany
Walking in Umbria
Walking Lake Garda and Iseo
Walking on the Amalfi Coast
Walking the Italian Lakes
Walks and Treks in the Maritime
   Alps

SCANDINAVIA

Walking in Norway

EASTERN EUROPE
AND THE BALKANS

The Danube Cycleway Vol 2
The High Tatras
The Mountains of Romania
Walking in Bulgaria's National
   Parks
Walking in Hungary
Mountain Biking in Slovenia
The Islands of Croatia
The Julian Alps of Slovenia
The Mountains of Montenegro
The Peaks of the Balkans Trail
The Slovenian Mountain Trail
Walking in Croatia
Walking in Slovenia: The
   Karavanke

SPAIN AND PORTUGAL

Coastal Walks in Andalucia
Cycle Touring in Spain
Cycling the Camino de Santiago
Mountain Walking in Mallorca
Mountain Walking in Southern
   Catalunya
Spain's Sendero Histórico: The
   GR1
The Andalucian Coast to Coast
   Walk
The Mountains of Nerja
The Mountains of Ronda and
   Grazalema
The Northern Caminos
The Sierras of Extremadura
Trekking in Mallorca
Walking and Trekking in the
   Sierra Nevada
Walking in Andalucia
Walking in Menorca
Walking in the Cordillera
   Cantabrica
Walking on Gran Canaria
Walking on La Gomera and El
   Hierro
Walking on La Palma
Walking on Lanzarote and
   Fuerteventura
Walking on Tenerife
Walking on the Costa Blanca
The Camino Portugués
Walking in Portugal
Walking in the Algarve
Walking on Madeira

GREECE, CYPRUS AND MALTA

The High Mountains of Crete
Trekking in Greece
Walking and Trekking in Zagori
Walking and Trekking on Corfu
Walking in Cyprus
Walking on Malta

INTERNATIONAL CHALLENGES,
COLLECTIONS AND ACTIVITIES

Canyoning in the Alps
Europe's High Points
The Via Francigena
   Canterbury to Rome – Part 2

AFRICA

Mountaineering in the Moroccan
   High Atlas
The High Atlas
Trekking in the Atlas Mountains
Walks and Scrambles in the
   Moroccan Anti-Atlas
Kilimanjaro
Walking in the Drakensberg

ASIA

Trekking in Tajikistan
Japan's Kumano Kodo Pilgrimage

Walking and Trekking in the
   Japan Alps and Mount Fuji
Jordan – Walks, Treks, Caves,
   Climbs and Canyons
Treks and Climbs in Wadi Rum,
   Jordan
Annapurna
Everest: A Trekker's Guide
Trekking in the Himalaya
Trekking in Bhutan
Trekking in Ladakh
The Mount Kailash Trek

NORTH AMERICA

British Columbia
The John Muir Trail
The Pacific Crest Trail

SOUTH AMERICA

Aconcagua and the Southern
   Andes
Hiking and Biking Peru's Inca
   Trails
Torres del Paine

TECHNIQUES

Fastpacking
Geocaching in the UK
Indoor Climbing
Lightweight Camping
Map and Compass
Outdoor Photography
Polar Exploration
Rock Climbing
Sport Climbing
The Mountain Hut Book

MINI GUIDES

Alpine Flowers
Avalanche!
Navigation
Pocket First Aid and Wilderness
   Medicine
Snow

MOUNTAIN LITERATURE

8000 metres
A Walk in the Clouds
Abode of the Gods
Fifty Years of Adventure
The Pennine Way – the Path, the
   People, the Journey
Unjustifiable Risk?

For full information on all our
guides, books and eBooks,
visit our website:
www.cicerone.co.uk

Walking – Trekking – Mountaineering – Climbing – Cycling

Over 40 years, Cicerone have built up an outstanding collection of over 300 guides, inspiring all sorts of amazing adventures.

 Every guide comes from extensive exploration and research by our expert authors, all with a passion for their subjects. They are frequently praised, endorsed and used by clubs, instructors and outdoor organisations.

All our titles can now be bought as **e-books**, **ePubs** and **Kindle** files and we also have an online magazine – **Cicerone Extra** – with features to help cyclists, climbers, walkers and trekkers choose their next adventure, at home or abroad.

Our website shows any **new information** we've had in since a book was published. Please do let us know if you find anything has changed, so that we can publish the latest details. On our **website** you'll also find great ideas and lots of detailed information about what's inside every guide and you can buy **individual routes** from many of them online.

It's easy to keep in touch with what's going on at Cicerone by getting our monthly **free e-newsletter**, which is full of offers, competitions, up-to-date information and topical articles. You can subscribe on our home page and also follow us on **Facebook** and **Twitter** or dip into our **blog**.

Cicerone – the very best guides for exploring the world.

CICERONE

Juniper House, Murley Moss, Oxenholme Road, Kendal, Cumbria LA9 7RL
Tel: 015395 62069 info@cicerone.co.uk
www.cicerone.co.uk